Eve Rozier

Thank you
for the love and support.
Blessings to you!

Glamorously
Yours,

GLAMOROUS SACRIFICE

GLAMOROUS
SACRIFICE

Life...
in the Shadow of Championships
Keva D. Horry

WHITE RIVER PRESS
AMHERST, MASSACHUSETTS

Glamorous Sacrifice
Life...in the Shadow of Championships

Published 2013 by White River Press, whiteriverpress.com

ISBN: 978-1-935052-32-6 (hardcover)
       978-1-935052-34-0 (paperback)

Credits:

Ferrell Phelps Photography - Houston, TX
Hargraves Photography - Houston, TX
Dana Eason Photography - Atlanta, GA

Book cover and graphic design:
Susan Jackson, the H2H studio - Huntsville, AL

Horry family home images

Disclaimer:

All third-party letters and other communication used by permission.

Library of Congress Cataloging-in-Publication Data

Horry, Keva DeVelle, 1971-
 Glamorous sacrifice / Keva DeVelle Horry.
     p. cm.
ISBN 978-1-935052-32-6 (hardcover : alk. paper) -- ISBN 978-1-935052-34-0 (pbk. : alk. paper)
1. Horry, Keva DeVelle, 1971- 2. Genetic disorders in children. 3. Mothers of children with disabilities--United States--Biography. 4. Athletes' spouses--United States--Biography. 5. National Basketball Association. I. Title.
 RJ47.3.H67 2010
 618.92'0042--dc22
                              2010021464

In loving memory of my father
Bernie A. DeVelle, Sr.

In loving honor and memory
of my beautiful baby girl
Ashlyn Ishan Horry

FOREWORD

Picture this...two NBA wives married to world-champion Los Angeles Lakers players, and we don't live with our husbands! Sounds crazy, right? Instead of living the full-time Hollywood life and basking in the glow of our mens' athletic success, Keva and I were running our households in other states far away. Keva in Houston, and me in New York. Keva and I would meet annually in the stands of the Staples Center with our children in tow (four for me; two for Keva). Each holiday we'd catch up on our lives, share stories about our kids, express our mutual dreams and comfort each other regarding our fears. We immediately connected due to our similar scenarios.

As life continued to change for both of us, our friendship remained the same. We are the kind of pals that listen, don't judge and comfort each other. Status, money or positions aren't an obstacle for us because we're the same woman. We are sisters with dreams, faults and strengths, and we are always in balance because of the gift of our wonderful kids.

While sharing a bond as Lakers wives, sitting next to each other in the arena stands cheering our husbands on game after game, there was a time when panic and despair was the flip side of our excitement. One incident in particular was in Houston, when I traveled to the city for an away game, and to hang out with Keva. We started our evening with the usual chatter about our kids, hubbies and fashion, but then she got an urgent call from home saying there was a problem with her daughter's feeding tube. Keva had to abruptly leave. As you'll soon find out, Keva has dealt with a tremendous set of circumstances surrounding her daughter who had special needs.

And therein lays our other bond as mothers, women and humanitarians. I have been part of the International Special Olympics board for nearly eight years. My invitation to join this tremendous movement was shortly after my participation in the "Very Special Christmas" album which allowed me to use my vocal talent to help spread the word about the impact the Special Olympics has on the world. Then I was asked by Maria Shriver to join as a board member and I was hooked. Interacting with the athletes, traveling the world to spread the word and truly being transformed through the success has allowed my life to change. I would sometimes feel helpless, that I wasn't making a difference because I was blessed with four children, and even though I could understand other parents' struggles, I hadn't personally gone through the specific struggle of raising a special-needs child.

I then got the opportunity to star in the film "My Brother." I played a mother with two sons - one with

Down Syndrome. We used two actors to portray the son with Down Syndrome (at younger and older ages). It was one of the most meaningful times in my life. I had the chance to step into that world for a few months.

Keva, however, championed that world daily. Children are our greatest achievements, and we would not be the people we are today without them. I am so blessed to have had the gift of giving birth four times. But Keva's journey as a mother, special-needs activist and fighter honestly blows me away. I am in awe of this dynamic force. She is wrapped in constant compassion and always wears a warm smile. I admire her undying strength and positive outlook on life in general, and that's exactly what you'll take away from experiencing her memoir, Glamorous Sacrifice.

We've traveled the world together, shared tears and shopped till we dropped. We've cooked on top of a mountain in Italy, salsa danced in Cuba and cruised down the Nile. We both even lost our loving fathers in the same year. Ours is a story of understanding, fortitude and faith. We share a belief that there is always a brighter day and the surrender that we don't always have the answers but that, eventually, they will come.

Enjoy Keva's journey as I have, and learn what made her the person she is today. She is remarkable.

Congratulations Keva!

Much love,

Vanessa Williams

CONTENTS

Introduction

I remember being in middle school, and the main focus in English class was to develop effective writing skills. This included writing book reports and journaling experiences. I hated it. I just hated writing. Ironically, my hatred of writing has yielded this book - gleaned from the many journals I've kept most of my adult life. Glamorous Sacrifice is a compilation of my years, fears and tears. It is also a celebration of my victories, defeats and milestones. This book is a tool by which I measure my growth, maturation, strength and confidence - all of which have deepened my faith and trust in God.

Today I love writing. It is an outlet for me to express myself without judgment. It has allowed me to articulate years of bottled emotions, to heal and to move forward. A major contributor to the aforementioned strength and growth is my beautiful daughter, Ashlyn Horry.

When I began writing this book, Ashlyn was a vibrant fifteen year old, a few weeks short of her sixteenth birthday. She was a divine angel who just loved people. She had a passion for life and love like I have never seen. I often call her my "love bunny." Ashlyn also had special needs, and she is the inspiration for this book.

Over the years, many people have asked, suggested and even insisted that I write a book about my experience being married to a celebrity (hence the word Glamorous), and raising a child with special needs (hence the word Sacrifice). Initially, I didn't think I had anything to say that would in any way impact the lives of others. I convinced myself no one would care, and remained cocooned in my comfortable, behind-the-scenes role as a wife and mother. But, it's hard to live in a cocoon when your spouse is a household name.

With the cocoon shattered, I then questioned whether or not my unique circumstances qualified as material for a real book. A pamphlet... maybe. I've shared my story in conversation many times, but to write a book...whoa.

My biggest fear when it came to writing this book, believe it or not, was crying. I just didn't want to cry anymore. I didn't want to revisit the past and relive its pain. However, by the grace of God, I was able to focus on the purpose of why I was reliving the painful moments. The purpose is to share with those who are ready to receive: the mother who is a caregiver like me; the single mom; the mom whose husband is away working to provide; the mom whose husband left because it was just "too much"; and of course, the mom who appears to have it all together but feels completely alone.

While my circumstances may not fit all of those molds, I can identify with pain and isolation. My situation included wealth (which separated me) and caring for my special-needs daughter (which consumed me). I couldn't talk to most people from a place of common familiarity. My social circle was small. My life was complicated and I was very young. I had the resources to do many things most never have the opportunity to do, but I usually couldn't engage because I had a beautiful daughter who needed everything I had to give her. That meant my time - which is everyone's most precious resource.

When I look at the person she became, I honor my decisions. So the tears are worth crying again because I know my life was designed to give hope and courage to other people. Our gifts are from God, and therefore are not to keep for ourselves for our own glory - they are to give away for His.

If there is one thing that I have learned about life, it is that no one is exempt from its challenges. Life does not discriminate based on race, creed, religion or economic status. Yet the beauty of life is that beneath the surface and tangible attachments, we are all more alike than we are different.

Ashlyn is a gift God gave me. She brought life to my purpose. She changed my life by giving me a different perspective. Ashlyn allowed me to view life from an unselfish, honest and compassionate lens. The saying "life is too short" is not a cliché. Life is too short. It's too short not to love hard, not to laugh loud and not to feel good with real gratitude. I can't imagine what my life would look like if I hadn't had Ashlyn. One thing is for sure, this book would never have been written had she not been born. I didn't get to this place overnight, but over the years grace has led me to this wonderful place of patience, understanding, compassion and humility. I could have easily cursed God, but I knew deep in my heart that He would not forsake me. As rough as the journey of motherhood has been for me, I can see His faithfulness and how He is using my life experiences to help enrich the lives of others. I believe whole-heartedly that the walk in victory comes when we persevere and stay patient in the journey - with a relentless quest to seize the victory Jesus died for us to possess. I believe that when Jesus said, "It is finished," He meant it. And everything is included in the word "It." Fear is finished. Pain is finished. Chaos is finished. Everything not of God is finished. It is up to us to make that Divine Truth a reality in every area of our lives.

This is not just a story; it's my story. It is a testament of long-suffering, hope and opportunity. And I give it to you, not to serve as a road map for your choices (if you share my situation), or as the answer to all of your questions. But rather, as a voice speaking to you...confirming that you are not alone.

It is my prayer and desire that no matter where you are in your life, that you take time to reflect on the truth that life is truly a gift. A gift none of us deserves, but that was lovingly, selflessly, sacrificially handed to us on a silver platter - by His grace.

Our individual destinations are relative. It's the process of the journey and our genuine appreciation of its purpose that matters. Thank you for allowing me to share and, hopefully, speak into your life. Enjoy!

~Keva D. Horry

GLAMOROUS SACRIFICE

CHAPTER ONE

Glamorous Background

"Life is not easy for any of us. But what of that?
We must have perseverance and above all confidence
in ourselves. We must believe that we are gifted for
something and that this thing must be obtained."
~Marie Curie

The spring of 1993 was an amazing time for me. I had just pledged a sorority at the university I was attending. Life couldn't get any better. At the close of the semester, I looked forward to returning to school in the fall to live my senior year in the sorority house with all my new sisters. I couldn't wait to attend the football games, engage in the activities on "the quad" with the other students and socialize outside the classroom. I was very much embracing the college experience. Of course, class attendance was included. I attended summer school. It was hot, just as every other Alabama summer had been. I remember walking to class one day and suddenly feeling nauseous. I was so nauseous that I broke into a sweat and began to feel weak. I knew I couldn't make it through class in this condition. I had just enough energy to make it back to the car and drive home.

When I walked in the house my dad asked, "Was class canceled?" I proceeded to the bathroom without saying a word and threw up. "Daddy, I don't feel good. I don't know what's wrong with me," I said. I had never felt that badly before, at least not that I could remember. He reminded me that I was dieting and that maybe eating tuna straight out of the can twice a day, mixed with the high humidity levels and scorching Alabama heat might, not be a feel-good recipe. Those factors hadn't dawned on me, but it made perfect sense. Since I had gotten a satisfactory diagnosis from Dr. Daddy, I figured I would just suffer through it, determined to lose the "freshman fifteen" I had gained three years earlier.

As I lay in bed with the air conditioner on full blast, I finally drifted off to sleep, only to be awakened an hour later by my sister (who is two years younger than me) hovering over me. She asked, "What's wrong with you?" I shouted at the top of my lungs, "I don't know. I just don't feel good. Now leave me alone!" (My sister and I share a closeness that no one understands; including the two of us at times.) She peered over my shoulder and prodded in a childish tone, "What's hurting you?" I said, "My stomach...now leave me alone!" Clearly dissatisfied with my dismissals, my sister once again pressed me, "You're not pregnant, are you?" I angrily answered, "I'm not pregnant. Now leave me alone!"

Little did my sister know, her question was like a song stuck on repeat. An internal dialogue - one that seemingly happened without my input - chirped away in my head. "I can't be. Or could I be? Nah, can't be. I'm about to start my cycle, right? Could I be?" This runaway conversation just made me sicker. I thought maybe if I started eating again as normal, all the sick feelings would go away. It seemed to be a great solution. But really, it was a function of denial.

After a week of eating normally, still feeling nauseous, and continuing to live in total denial, I decided to take a home pregnancy test. Of course, I couldn't do it alone, so I called on the support of my girlfriend and former roommate to accompany me in purchasing *the test*.

We went to her apartment. In the event *the test* was positive and I had a nervous breakdown, I felt less stressed there than at home with my father...who I imagined would not be able to hide his extreme disappointment. I finally mustered the courage to go to the bathroom and "anoint" the stick that would tell me my fate. After twenty minutes of anxiety-ridden waiting (even though it took just five minutes for the results to appear), I dropped to the floor sobbing uncontrollably. The plus sign on *the test* seemed to be in bold type, underlined, italicized and magnified. I was pregnant. I felt shock, denial, anger, fear and temporary insanity all at once. I couldn't fathom how to begin to process everything. I couldn't really think about my senior year of college - which was right in front of me. Days before *the test*, I was consumed with thoughts of graduating, celebrating and every other major milestone associated with one's senior year in college. But after *the test*, all I could focus on was how disappointed my father was going to be. I was a true daddy's girl. I didn't know how to fix this one at all. Abortion was not an option, period (pardon the pun). Although, falling off the face of the earth rather than facing my father about the pregnancy would have been just fine with me.

I spent two days at my girlfriend's apartment before deciding to go home to tell my parents the news. My parents were divorced, so I chose to tell them separately. I told my father first. I went to his home and told him I needed to share something with him. We sat across from each other in the formal living room. My heart was racing and tears were falling before I could even speak. He asked me what was wrong. With crocodile tears still falling, I told my father that all of the nausea I had been experiencing wasn't from a combination of dieting and Alabama's summer heat and humidity.

"I took a pregnancy test and I am pregnant," I blurted out.

I told him my plan to finish school, and that I never meant to disappoint him. The news definitely came as a total shock to him, but he was merciful and loving. His first response was a brief Biblical lesson. Then he told me he was glad I was twenty-two years old and not a teenage mother-to-be. He wanted me to keep my promise to finish school. He said I'd come too far not to complete my degree. He also wanted to talk with my boyfriend and me together. He wanted to hear from him what his plans were now that we had created another life. He hugged me, told me he loved me and that everything was going to be all right. For whatever reason, all the anxiety I was feeling left me. I guess my dad's assurance of love and security made all the difference.

Next up, my mother. I went to her house, and we sat in the den. I shared the news with her the same way I had with my father. She didn't have quite the same reaction he did. She was in total denial. She didn't believe me. In fact, she said, "Keva, that's nothing to joke about. You shouldn't play like that." She looked in my eyes as I said, "Mom, I'm not playing. I really am pregnant." I'm not sure she believed me until I actually started showing months later. After getting it out in the open, the rest of that day was a blur, but the worst of it was over.

During the two days spent at my girlfriend's apartment before facing my parents, I made every anxious attempt to get in touch with my boyfriend, who I met and started dating in April 1991. He was out of town at the time. Now, when I say he was "out of town," what I actually mean is he was living out of town. After a successful collegiate career, my then-boyfriend, Robert Horry, was drafted in 1992 and began his professional basketball career in the National Basketball Association (NBA) with the Houston Rockets. We were managing our long-distance relationship, which was difficult. We both agreed that, while we wanted to be together, Robert's future and career as a professional basketball player was equally as important as our relationship. We were willing to sacrifice living in the same town while I finished school and he focused on establishing himself with his team.

I finally did get in touch with him. To my chagrin, he was thrilled when I told him the news. I thought he was crazy. Like my parents' reactions, his was not at all what I'd anticipated. I thought he would try to talk me out of having the baby, use the unexpected pregnancy as an excuse to split and move on to the next woman. On one hand, I was very grateful that did not happen. On the other hand, I knew the only person's life that was really going to change was mine. In fact, it already had. From the moment I learned I was pregnant, my hopes and dreams seemed to be instantly dead. It had been a longtime dream of mine to be the next Connie Chung (the *CBS Evening News* anchorwoman at that time). I watched the *CBS Evening News* faithfully. After completing an internship at the local news station (which happened to be the *CBS* affiliate in my town) during my junior year in college, I often stood in the mirror speaking into my hairbrush or curling iron, repeating things Connie said and pretending I was delivering the news to the national public. I figured if she could succeed as an anchor being a woman and a minority, I could do it too.

Well, Connie went on to the next phase of her life, and so did I. I eventually realized that, even though my life had taken a major detour, it was not over. After lots of open discussion, prayer and weighing the pros and cons, I also learned that my hopes and dreams were also still very much alive (albeit indefinitely on-hold). One thing I treasure about my life's experiences is the fact that absolutely nothing can take the place of love and support from my family - regardless of the circumstances.

So that is how I began my senior year in college: pregnant, receiving a lot of support from my family and establishing a new dedication and continued hope for a bright, promising future. I moved into the sorority house. Things got off to a very sweet start. Robert drove from his new home in Houston, Texas to my sorority house in Tuscaloosa, Alabama and proposed marriage. I initially gave him a hard time. I wanted to make sure he was proposing to me for the "right" reasons, and not because I was expecting his child. We loved each other very much and marriage had been a topic of discussion. We definitely knew marriage was in our future, but being pregnant changed everything. I began to doubt his love for me. I felt afraid and insecure - two emotions I had never allowed in my life. Up until that point, everything I approached or encountered was met with my excitement and willingness. But from the moment I found out I was pregnant, I suddenly distrusted my own judgment. I wasn't sure if he would still love me for me, or if the baby would change his feelings toward me. Realizing that a marriage proposal is a vulnerable moment (for a man especially), I was very open with Robert about my fears, thoughts and feelings. After a long discussion and a solid reassurance of his love for me, as well as mine for him, he took my left hand and placed a beautiful princess cut diamond ring on my ring finger. In love, pregnant and engaged... now *that's* change!

Speaking of changes, being pregnant also made a stranger of the body chemistry I'd always known. I was always sick. The sicker I got, the more afraid I became. It was August. The baby was due the end of March. I was determined to get through that semester of school. However, determination apparently wasn't enough. Between morning sickness and getting the flu (what fun!), it took all the energy I had just to get out of bed, take a shower and put on clean pajamas (only to get right back in bed). All the sickness I was experiencing meant I was missing a lot of class. I didn't want failing grades on my transcript. So, by the middle of October 1993, I made the extremely difficult decision to withdraw from school and return after the baby was born. By the time I'd made this decision, I was still very sick and a little depressed because the excitement about school that once consumed me no longer existed. I knew somehow I would have to shift the excitement from my future as a college graduate to the future that lay just ahead - wife and Mom. I also had to keep repeating the fact that my life was not over. It was just different than what I'd planned. Drastically different.

I went out with a bang. My sorority sisters hosted my very first baby shower at the sorority house. It was bittersweet. The shower itself was lovely, and I was delighted they were sharing in that special time with me. Nevertheless, I couldn't help but think about how much

I would miss them, and what could have been if I didn't have to leave. My friends and sorority sisters stayed in close contact with me even though I wasn't on campus anymore. Still weak from pregnancy illness, I was receiving very good prenatal care. Of course, everyone knows there are very few medications an expectant mother can take. Tylenol for discomfort maybe, but not too much more. I opted not to even take Tylenol. The flu had to run its course. Once it had, I was bursting with energy. Things were looking up.

Hindsight, as the saying goes, is always 20/20. As I look back over this period of time, I recall that at one of my regular doctor visits my doctor gave me the option to get an amniocentesis. There was no cause for concern, at least not that he shared with me. He just mentioned the procedure as an available option, explained what it was and asked if I'd like to have it done. I went home and told my mom what the doctor said. She was actually upset he would even mention such a thing considering I was only twenty-two years old. She said physicians usually give that particular test to much older women. Having had three children, I was sure my mom was knowledgeable on the subject. Since the doctor had given no reason to be concerned about anything, I opted not to have a long needle stuck in my stomach.

My mom was unsettled about the mention of my getting an amniocentesis, and wanted me to get a second opinion. I ended up changing physicians. My new doctor confirmed there was still no reason for concern, and that he understood my mom's position. From her perspective I was twenty-two years old; not forty-two years old. Her logic was, if there was no reason for concern, why go to such an extreme? After the physician switch and more intense discussion, I made the final decision not to have the procedure done. Robert and I talked three-to-five times a day every day. That had become our norm. He was very good about wanting the details of my prenatal doctor visits. His support meant the world to me. After a while, the long distance relationship had begun to take its toll on the both of us - especially me.

On February 1, 1994, at eight months pregnant and with my physician's consent, I moved to Houston to be with him. Traveling with me were my Dad and my unborn angel, Ashlyn. We loaded the SUV with all my belongings and my Dad drove us to Texas. What would normally be an eight-hour drive turned into a very unpleasant eleven-hour one. Between all the restroom stops and food stops, I'm sure I got on my Dad's final nerve. This was a compounded irritation, by the way. My Dad was not happy about my moving to Texas, so I'm sure the frequent potty and food breaks on the drive there were really adding insult to injury for him. My mother wasn't thrilled about my moving either, but she knew I was an adult and she lovingly supported me. At the end of the day, so did my Dad. They were my parents. We all had to face the fact that this wasn't quite the scenario – or the order of events - any of us had envisioned for me. Nevertheless, it was what it was, and they were a solid rock for me. The bottom line was that I had to focus on the present. I was excited to be reunited with the love of my life. Little did I know, I was about to embark on one more thing that would (once again) create a massive shift in my world. The love of my life was about to make history in his sport.

Two days after arriving in Houston, a very significant NBA trade was made. That trade is now often referred to as "The trade that wasn't." The Houston Rockets were trading Robert (who was a first-round draft pick) and his teammate Matt Bullard for first-round draft pick Sean Elliot (who played for the Detroit Pistons). My first thought was about what I was going to do. I was beyond pregnant. I couldn't move again. I was in the last trimester of my pregnancy, and I had already begun having contractions as a result of the long drive from Alabama to Texas. Robert had to report to Detroit right away. He was on a plane that afternoon. Everything was in question. We had gone from being excited to be with one another (and him bonding with the baby), to this abrupt uprooting. We were both hurt and frustrated for various reasons. I remember pacing the floor, crying and praying that God would work the situation out.

God delivered.

After the trade was official, it was then announced that it had been rescinded. For the first time in Houston Rockets NBA history, a trade of that magnitude didn't go through.

Sean Elliot had issues with his kidneys and did not pass his physical. As soon as the news surfaced, Robert was on a plane headed back to Houston. With all due respect to Sean, my prayers were answered. That trade was not meant to be.

Robert was back home with a new attitude. At last, I could concentrate on what was new and in the future. Making the adjustment to a new place was one thing, but making that adjustment in a major metropolitan city was quite another. Houston is enormous compared to my Alabama hometown of Tuscaloosa (Roll Tide!). Everything in Houston was enormous. I quickly learned that the familiar saying, "Everything's bigger in Texas" is not a cliché. It's pure fact. I learned to get to the grocery store, the OBGYN and back home. I couldn't venture out too far, as I didn't want to get stuck somewhere on the side of the freeway in labor. For the most part, I could adjust to change fairly easily, but this was different. I believe for the first time ever, I was genuinely afraid. It wasn't like I had not traveled or been away from my parents (I'd even traveled abroad). What made it different was that I was officially away from home (as I defined "home") and was creating a new one. What also made it different was that I was about to start a life of my own - a family of my own. I was twenty-two years old and I didn't have a clue as to what life had in store for me.

CHAPTER TWO

GLAMOROUS ARRIVAL

"A woman is the full circle. Within her is the power to create, nurture, and transform."
~Diane Mariechild

My "nesting period" had come and gone. The baby nursery was prepared with all the trimmings - complete with the mural on the wall and the matching comforter in her crib. All the baby clothes were washed, folded and put away. Picture frames were in place waiting for the beautiful face of my baby girl. My bag was packed and at the door. I was ready to go to the hospital and bring my baby into the world.

At forty weeks gestation I was more than ready to deliver. After three false labor alarms, I didn't think she would ever come. Ashlyn showed evidence of her strong will even before her grand arrival. After the third false alarm, the doctor admitted me into the hospital. I was about to be a Mommy. It was surreal. I had no idea what to expect with the delivery process. I'd taken the birthing classes, but I now realize those classes didn't prepare me for what I actually went through. The timing of the contractions grew closer together. I had dilated to the point that it was too late to receive an epidural. My doctor kept saying, "Keva, you're doing just fine. Wonderful. You're almost there. You don't need the epidural." I was dazed, having contractions, in major pain and breathing as if there was a global oxygen shortage, but there was nothing wrong with my hearing. I remember thinking, "Did he just say what I think he said?" After I realized he had, I did something totally uncharacteristic of me. I yelled back at that man and said, "Get me the drugs!" Now to be very clear, I was not trying to be Superwoman, and I don't love needles, but I was experiencing a specific pain he would *never* experience, and I was not open to his suggestion that I didn't need the epidural! The thought of a needle piercing my back unnerved me then and now. My stern request for the epidural was not an emotionally driven whim...I needed it! So, due to my shrieking demand, my doctor agreed to my having the epidural. It took two nurses to hold me so the anesthesiologist could administer it. Their only mistake was allowing me to see the needle. Between the pain from the contractions and the glaring reality of that incredibly long needle going into my back, I was ready to jump off the table and run. Millions of thoughts were going through my head with every second that passed. Not to frighten all the future Mom's out there, but I was in severe, mind-blowing pain...and I was scared. I was yelling for my Momma (yep, I wanted my Momma when I was about to become one), and I held on to every nurse in the room with a grip they are likely still feeling today.

I had heard about the water breaking just before delivery. Each time I heard about it, I automatically thought of cool spring water.

I was more than wrong in that thinking.

My water breaking was the surprise of my life. The epidural needle went in, and the water (which was not cool) came out - at the same time. I thought I was dying. The nurses obviously knew this was normal and they met my horror with the nonchalant "business as usual" approach only nurses can execute. I was the biggest whining, crying, moaning, groaning baby to ever set foot in a maternity ward. I'm sure the nurses wanted to laugh at me, but I didn't care.

The contractions got closer. I knew there was no turning back. The epidural had kicked in, but I still felt pain. The nurses called it "pressure." Nice try. It was *pain* and I was extremely uncomfortable. It left me wondering if they gave me the entire dosage, considering that the doctor was trying his best not to give it to me at all. At last, it was time to get the show on the road. After several loud commands for me to push, our daughter made her debut.

On April 2, 1994 at 4:55 P.M., Ashlyn Ishan Horry was born at 5 pounds, 5.6 ounces and 18 ½ inches long at West Houston Memorial Hospital. She had ten fingers, ten toes and a head full of long, beautiful, black, curly hair. I was overcome by a whirlwind of emotions: joy, happiness, anticipation, marvel and fear. I have no problem admitting my almost paralyzing fear at the thought of a living, breathing little person coming out of me. Robert wasn't there for Ashlyn's birth (which contributed to my fear). Ironically, he was playing a game with the Rockets in Los Angeles against the Lakers - a team with which he would later win three NBA championships. Thankfully though, I was not alone. My mother and Robert's mother, Lelia, were with me.

As soon as Ashlyn was born, the doctor put her in my arms. I looked at her and she opened her eyes. Most people would consider that among one of their most cherished life moments. Me? Not so much. That moment freaked me out. To this day, I still have no idea why. All I know is that in that moment, I remembered all the women who had shared with me (while I was pregnant) their joyful birthing experiences. But when Ashlyn opened her eyes, I wasn't sharing their joy. Now, the *idea* of what I'd heard all those women describe was wonderful. But ideas and actuality are not always one in the same. My experience of the birthing process was terrifying. I found it interesting that I never heard the word "terrifying" from any of those women...seems a big detail to omit! I was lying in a hospital bed coming to terms with the fact that I actually had to take my baby home and take care of her. I knew I had strong nurturing tendencies and a loving heart. After all, I had a brother ten years my junior, and I took care of him regularly when he was a baby. In fact, I remembered that he would get fussy at naptime. When he wouldn't go to sleep for my parents, they would petition me, "The Baby Whisperer," to impart my Midas touch. Nevertheless, as fond as those memories were, I knew none of that meant I was ready for a baby of my own.

Then a mental memo arrived in my brain's inbox: *It's too late for doubt and questions now, Keva. She's here.* Just after the mental memo, the reality check landed. I didn't know the first thing about taking care of a baby. I felt nauseous (again) and was about to throw up. I quickly gave the baby to my mother and proceeded to projectile vomit across the room.

Real cute. Not exactly this southern belle's finest hour.

Apparently, the epidural was wearing off and nausea was one of the side effects. (In my opinion, the full effect of the epidural never happened.) Again, a key piece of information everyone conveniently forgot to mention. Just after I spewed my guts and added my input regarding the room's décor (not that anyone asked for it), I became instantly convinced that every woman who had freely chosen to give birth more than once was certifiably insane. That was some serious pain to endure. I thought, "Why would anyone in their right mind put themselves through this - intentionally - after they'd lived through it once?" That was my twenty-three-year-old mindset. Thank God for maturity!

I felt much better after my projectile "cleanse." During my Picasso impression, the nurse had taken Ashlyn to the nursery for clean up, preparing to bring her back so I could nurse her for the first time. I was very nervous about that as well, but I wanted to take the healthiest avenues possible for my daughter. I was more than willing to put all apprehensions aside for her (those "Mommy" instincts sure did kick in quickly.)

While they were cleaning her up, I decided to call my relatives and friends back home to let them know Ashlyn had finally arrived (I spared them the gory details I have not spared you!). I was so engrossed in my conversations, I didn't realize how much time had passed since Ashlyn had been taken out of the room. A few hours had gone by. I was certain she must have been hungry. I pushed the call button for the nurse. A voice yelled from the other end that someone would be right there. I started to feel in my gut that something was terribly wrong. Lelia and my mom - who had left to go to the nursery - came back in. Both of them had disturbing looks on their faces, but neither of them said a word. I asked, "What's wrong? Where is Ashlyn?" They said nothing. My heart started to race. I tried as best I could to sit up in the bed. Shouting this time, I asked again, "Where is Ashlyn?" Lelia told me the doctor was coming in to talk to me. The fact that she was alluding to something being wrong, but deferring to the doctor to tell me what was wrong, was disturbing and frightening. My heart dropped.

I said, "What do you mean? Talk to me about what?" Just then, the doctor and the nurse walked in. I sat up even taller in the bed, adjusting the pillows behind my back. "What is wrong? Tell me what's going on. Please!" The doctor asked me to calm down. His next words were the most dreadful words a mother (especially a new mother) never wants to hear.

"Your daughter is having difficulty breathing. We are not sure what is causing this to happen, so we need to send her to another hospital. We will be transporting her by ambulance to Texas Children's Hospital immediately." He continued, "I wish I had more answers for you. As soon as we get her to the other hospital, we will learn more." I started crying uncontrollably. I don't ever recall feeling so empty or having such an overwhelming sense of loneliness. The birth of our daughter was supposed to be a happy occasion. Nothing bad was supposed to happen. Ashlyn coming into this world was supposed to be a perfect, incident-free experience. I looked at my mom and Lelia. They were also crying, but trying to find words to comfort me. Lelia kept Robert updated of every detail via telephone. He was due back in Houston later that night. I was consumed with unspeakable heaviness. Lelia eventually told me (much later) that as she and my mother were standing outside the nursery window looking eagerly for Ashlyn, the nurse walked to the viewing window and closed the blinds. As they tried to peer through the cracks of the closed blinds, they realized something was terribly wrong. Lelia said my mother immediately called home for my family to start a prayer chain for Ashlyn. I was surprised to hear about the nurses shutting the blinds, but not at all surprised to hear about my mother initiating corporate prayer, as I come from a long, strong line of Christian prayer warriors. Ashlyn definitely wasn't going to make it through that situation without prayer, and neither was I.

After much debate between the doctor and me about my getting an immediate discharge to be with Ashlyn at Texas Children's Hospital rather than staying overnight, I won. There was no way I was going to be at one hospital with her several miles away at another hospital, alone and fighting for her life. I was determined to be there for her and with her. Without having any answers to my many questions, I was on my way to be with my baby.

My doctor was very concerned about my health, and rightfully so. I had just given birth a few hours prior to Ashlyn's transport. Childbirth makes the body very vulnerable, and the recuperation period is vital to a woman's overall health. Nevertheless, none of those facts were on my mind at the time. Ashlyn was my focus.

Everything was happening so fast. Suddenly, I was having trouble breathing. I felt anxious and agitated. My head began to throb. My body felt heated and started to pulsate. I didn't know what was happening to me, but I couldn't (and wouldn't) take the time to find out. If I had said anything, it would have only delayed my plan of getting to my daughter. I was on a mission. With discharge papers in one hand and the other hand waving goodbye to the nurses, I was wheeled out of the hospital to my SUV where Lelia was waiting to take me to Ashlyn. My mother was not far behind, pushing a cart filled with all the flowers, balloons, stuffed animals and other gifts I received while in the hospital. Robert's mother assisted the nurses with getting me into the car. Once I was in with my seatbelt buckled, I looked over my left shoulder. My eyes quickly focused and fixated on the empty car seat that was lovingly prepared to carry Ashlyn home for the first time. I could barely swallow because of the lump in my throat.

As we rode from one hospital to the other, there was no conversation and no music - only road noise. I wept quietly as I was driven to the world-renowned Texas Children's Hospital - without my daughter, without answers and without any perspective.

I had no idea that the world-renowned hospital would become my home for the next six months.

CHAPTER THREE

Glamorous Stay...
In Neonatal Intensive Care Unit

"In the middle of difficulty lies opportunity."
~Albert Einstein

As I entered the unit, I heard loud, piercing sounds. I felt as if I was in another world. It was foreign to me. There were continuous beeping noises. The ear-splitting pitches came from the monitors attached to each infant in the unit. Each monitor had a conductor used to establish electrical contact with a nonmetallic circuit part known as electrodes. The monitors would alert the nurses when heart rates were dropping, temperatures were rising or oxygen levels were decreasing. I had a lump in my throat. I had never seen anything like that before. The unit was set up in pods, and each pod held between four and six infants, depending on how many sick babies there were at the time. I was directed to Ashlyn's pod. As I walked closer to her little bed, I heard loud breathing, as if an adult was doing the breathing for her. I got a bit closer. "Oh Dear Father," I said, as my eyes welled with tears. I was not ready for what I was seeing. Ashlyn was what they called "intubated." The medical definition for that is the introduction of a tube into a hollow organ (such as the trachea or an intestine) to either keep it open or to restore its patency (if it is obstructed). In other words, there was a long tube in her tiny mouth holding her airway open while a machine gave her oxygen. The positioning of the tube was supported with tape around her mouth, which nearly covered the entire lower half of her small face. She had an I.V. placed in the top of her hand, and a feeding tube was threaded through her nose to her tummy. I felt so helpless. I had no indication of that moment being the beginning of a long journey. Once again, my life was taking a drastic turn.

Robert arrived in Houston at around midnight and headed straight for the hospital from the airport. On doctor's orders, I had been sent home to rest. I wanted to talk to Robert before he got to the hospital so I could prepare him for what he was going to see. My best efforts to do that failed. A sadness came over me when I realized he was going to see Ashlyn without any kind of mental preparation. I wanted to be there with him. He called to let me know that he had seen her and was on his way home. The tone in his voice was solemn. I had no words, yet I was anxious to see him and hold him. I was longing to be held, as well. Neither of us understood what was going on. We didn't know the why's or the how's. There were so many unanswered questions. That night we simply held each other and went to sleep.

The next day my head was still throbbing and I continued to experience the pulsating feeling throughout my body. I had no energy, and I was just not feeling well at all. It was definitely time to get my doctor involved. When I called him, he instructed me to come to his office immediately. Robert drove me to the doctor's office, and stayed with me for my evaluation. I learned that my blood pressure had skyrocketed and I was on the verge of a fatal situation. Robert and I were terrified. Now, you should note that Robert doesn't scare easily - he's generally pretty steady and laid back - so the fact that he was freaked out made me all the more fearful. So now we're in a panic about Ashlyn's *and* my health.

The doctor advised me not to leave his office until my blood pressure stabilized. If it didn't stabilize, he said he would send me to the nearest ER. As I lay there in a dimly lit room on the cold table with a pillow under my head and my feet elevated, Robert began making jokes and reflecting on old times. Because joking is one of his coping mechanisms, he mistakenly thought that would relax me. Despite the "A" I gave him for effort, his eyes filled with tears. As fearful as I was, I knew I had to be strong. After all, I had a child to raise. I told him, "I'm not going anywhere. You're not getting rid of me that easily!"

The physical stress of giving birth and the emotional stress of actually seeing Ashlyn struggling for her life had taken a toll on me. My brain was telling me one thing: that I was fine and I needed to focus on my daughter. But my body was saying something completely different: that I had just delivered a baby – who was fighting for her life - and I was traumatized. We were in the OB/GYN's office for nearly four hours. The staff had left for the day. My doctor was very thorough and made certain that my blood pressure was under control before sending me home. I was grateful for him. Had I let those symptoms continue without seeking medical supervision, I wouldn't be here to talk or write about it. That's how far into the danger zone I'd gotten. He put me on bed rest for two days, which meant I couldn't get to the hospital to see Ashlyn. Those were the two longest days of my life. My mom and Lelia alternated going to the hospital. One would stay with me, and the other with Ashlyn; calling me with updates on her status and delivering messages from the doctors who had seen her. There was not much news to report. There were more questions being asked about family medical history than answers being given in response to our questions.

At this time, we lived in a suburb of Houston called Sugar Land. This was about twenty-five miles from the Medical Center, which houses Texas Children's Hospital. Once I was out of medical danger and on my feet, I made that drive to town every day. I was eager to see my daughter, and disappointed when there was no change in her status. We were not told how much longer Ashlyn would be in the Neonatal Intensive Care Unit (NICU). The doctors tested her constantly. She was still on the breathing machine and being fed through a feeding tube. I would pump my breasts, and take the milk to the hospital every day. I wanted her to feel that nurturing closeness with me – in some way - since she would never nurse directly from me. I cannot put into words the intense helplessness I felt every time I looked at her lying there in that baby bed. While staring blankly at her, I would often wonder what happened and where things went wrong.

These were the days when Robert was on the road with the team and I was mostly home alone. My mom and Lelia returned to their respective homes (in Tennessee and Alabama) after I'd recovered enough to function on my own. They were both working as teachers and had to return to work. When they left, Robert's father (Robert Sr.) visited for a few weeks to help take care of me. I was still healing, and needed the company while Robert was on the road with the Rockets. Many times, I would be at the hospital with Ashlyn all day and leave for home in the wee hours of the morning. There were also times I would stay at the hotel across the street from the hospital because Robert didn't want me driving home that late by myself. Then there were the days when I would stay all day and all night, only leaving her side to eat or go to the bathroom. I was determined for Ashlyn to know, without question, that I was her mother. I would touch her little hands, kiss her tiny feet and rub her little arms and legs. I wanted her to know my touch. I talked to her. I sang songs to her. I prayed over her. If she knew anyone's voice, she knew mine. The reality of being a new mother in a strange new city resonated heavily with me. I didn't know very many people in Houston. The few people I did know were associated with the Rockets. Robert and Ashlyn represented the only family I had in Houston. I was starting to feel the impact of this reality. It was clear that my support system would accumulate a lot of frequent flier miles.

It was odd having Robert's father - rather than my mom - take care of me after giving birth. However, he did it well. He cooked and did household chores. My favorite memory with him is the morning doughnut runs he would make for breakfast. He was so thoughtful. I didn't want for anything. He took care of me as if I were his own daughter.

Everyone within our support system visited in shifts. When Robert's dad had to leave, my dad came and stayed for extended periods. The first three months of Ashlyn's NICU stay were long and grueling as we were still anxiously awaiting the specifics about her situation. Countless tests had been done, and the doctors still had no answers. Robert and I had given blood and had been swabbed for DNA testing to determine if there were any abnormal chromosomes in our genetics that could have been passed on to her. That answer, thankfully, was no. We were questioned about our family medical histories, and whether or not anyone in the family had abnormal chromosomes or some sort of genetic complications. There weren't. We asked the doctor if Ashlyn's condition was because of something we did, or if there was something that went overlooked in gestation that could have been detected. We wanted to know how it happened.

But, the doctors were still uncertain and hesitant to make assumptions about a diagnosis, much less a prognosis. Weeks into this battle, Robert and I still had very few answers and our patience was growing thin. I remember getting angry because it seemed that every time I turned around the nurses were either sticking her little fingers and/or toes to draw blood for testing (every day), or introducing a new I.V. in a new location. She cried and cried. I cried and cried. The helplessness I felt was suffocating. Ashlyn had been given a substantial amount of medication intravenously at this point, and all of the veins in her hands, arms and on top of her feet had been used. The heels of her feet looked like pincushions. Because all her veins had been used, the last resort was to shave her head and use the larger veins there - which, to my horror, they did. When that plan expired, the doctors surgically inserted a Central Line in Ashlyn. A Central Line is an I.V. line inserted into a large vein (typically in the neck or near the heart) to administer medicines or fluids, or to withdraw blood. Ashlyn's Central Line was near her heart. The scar from that procedure was a constant reminder of that frightening and somber time: a time when she lay motionless on her back. I remember purchasing a Fisher Price tape recorder. I taped myself singing and reading stories to Ashlyn. On the rare occasions when I was home long enough to sleep in my own bed, I made arrangements for the tape to be played so she would know I was always there, and that she wasn't alone. Day after day, Ashlyn lay in that tiny bed entangled in multiple cords: from electrodes to feeding tubes to the pulse oximeter (a sensor that measures oxygen saturation of the blood) to the I.V. It took continuous effort to situate the cords and keep them from tangling so I could hold her and enable her to feel the warmth of my body and the beat of my heart.

As doctors diligently worked for a resolution and the scenario continued to unravel, it was discovered that the main component of Ashlyn's many issues was Laryngomalacia. This was the cause of her not being able to breathe properly and requiring administered oxygen. Laryngomalacia is excess tissue surrounding the epiglottis. Her "overgrown epiglottis" had a mind of its own. At any given time it would get "lazy" and collapse, causing her airway to shut off and inhibit her breathing. Dr. Ellen Friedman, Ear, Nose and Throat (ENT) surgeon at Texas Children's Hospital performed a series of laser surgeries to slowly diminish the excess tissue, hoping the breathing issues would be solved. After the surgeries though, it was certain Ashlyn was not safe. She still had to be intubated and was not out of danger. This was, obviously, a major disappointment for Robert and me. The doctor asked us to consider allowing her to perform a tracheostomy: the surgical procedure forming an opening into Ashlyn's trachea (through her neck), allowing the passage of air. I could not believe what was happening. I could not believe I had to make these decisions for my daughter. I would rather have been deciding which hair bow matched her dress, or which baby shoes she would wear.

Dr. Friedman wanted to make sure we understood all that was involved with the tracheostomy procedure, so we visited other kids in the hospital who had had the procedure. I was, once again, terrified. I quickly learned that my fear - in that particular case - was the byproduct of ignorance. The kids we saw were warriors, and I left our visits with them feeling nothing but admiration for them and determination for Ashlyn. I had to learn how to keep the tracheostomy site from getting infected. I had to learn how to keep Ashlyn from getting water in the tracheostomy site, as water in the site meant easy access of water to her lungs (which was incredibly dangerous). I had to learn to insert a plastic device (the trache) for periodic replacement. I had to learn to use a suction device to remove mucus and saliva, which she could not clear herself by coughing like most people. I needed to visit these kids.

After the visits and processing the new information, we gave the green light for the tracheostomy. Approximately three weeks after that surgery, she underwent another surgery performed by Pediatric Surgeon, Dr. Paul Minifee. That surgery was to insert a *G-button* - a small plastic device in her stomach that uses tubing attachments for feeding. That surgery also included a fundoplication - a surgical procedure where the upper portion of the stomach is wrapped around the lower end of the esophagus and sutured in place as a treatment for reflux of stomach contents into the esophagus.

Because Ashlyn had such difficulty breathing on her own, it was also difficult for her to eat. The G-button would allow her to feed and get all of the nutrients she needed whether she was taking a bottle by mouth or not. We realized after the G-button insertion surgery that Ashlyn was experiencing different symptoms we hadn't seen. The new symptoms were being diagnosed, but our primary question still remained: what was the source of *all* the symptoms? The inevitable waiting during this time presented a defining lesson for me. I learned that there are times in life when fears have to take a backseat to action - especially when someone's life depends on it. And that is what I did, for Ashlyn's sake.

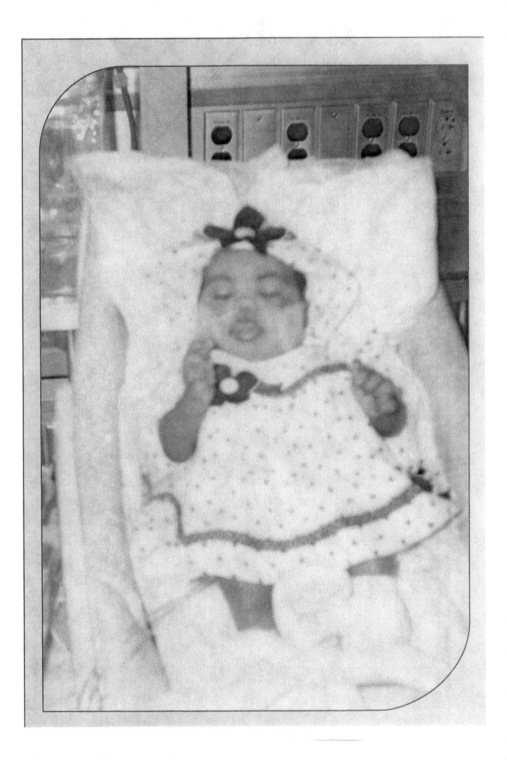

CHAPTER FOUR

Glamorous News

"Man can learn nothing except by going from
the known to the unknown."
~Claude Bernard

The "clutch city" Houston Rockets were on the road once again. Accompanied by my father while visiting Ashlyn at the hospital, I was approached at her bedside by a doctor who requested to speak with us in "the room." This particular room was where the physicians would take families to talk with them before or after fatal situations. During the three month period we had already spent in the NICU, I witnessed several families enter "the room," but I never saw them return to the hospital. I could not believe it was my turn to go in there. I had the biggest lump in my throat (again), and I felt it would suffocate me. "This cannot be happening," I thought. My heart was pounding. Every thought that could have possibly gone through my head did - in milliseconds. I kept holding on to the fact that Ashlyn was still alive. Several doctors had spoken to me earlier while I was with her in the unit. Why was this time so different? I was reluctant to cross the threshold of "the room," but I wanted answers. I slowly walked in, and as I did, I could feel a coldness come over me. Dry mouth. Numb feet. Clammy hands. Overwhelming anxiety had crept in. My dad followed directly behind me. The room was dimly lit. I wondered what that meant. Was it to serve as comfort on some level? There was a sofa on my left, where my dad and I sat, and a coffee table directly in front of us. Conveniently, a box of Kleenex was positioned in the center of the coffee table. A team of surgeons, geneticists and resident doctors filed into the room. All I remember to this day is a sea of white coats standing at attention in front of me. Being called into "the room" was intimidating enough. I couldn't focus on their faces. I felt as if I could have been knocked over with a feather.

I will never forget what happened next.

The spokesperson for the group began some semblance of an explanation about what was happening with our daughter's health. I understood him to say that Ashlyn had a very rare chromosome abnormality, which had caused a multitude of problems for her. "It is a partial deletion of her number one chromosome," he said. He continued explaining that, because of the rarity of the condition, they were not able to offer much additional information with respect to a prognosis. He told me things were not looking good for Ashlyn. She had Laryngomalacia, which we all thought would be successfully resolved with surgery. She had a G-button placed in her stomach so she could sustain nourishment and a fundoplication to cease the reflux. She had a kidney condition called Renal Tubular Acidosis (RTA). She suffered from severe sleep apnea and they had also discovered irregular heart patterns. At this point, the doctor knelt down by the coffee table (as if that would increase my understanding) and said, "*If* your daughter lives beyond this point, she will be mentally retarded. She may not have the facial distortion, but she will definitely be considered mentally retarded. She will have learning disabilities, and more than likely will not be able to walk or talk." He added softly, "I want you to know that there was nothing you or your husband could have done differently. This was just a freak accident of nature."

Well, so much for being consoled. It was somewhere between the word "freak" and the word "accident" that the anxiety left me. The anxiety left me because I'd heard the worst, and I was already shifting to survival mode. Nevertheless, it's nearly two decades later, and I've yet to completely digest those words. Hearing this news at twenty-three years old was devastating. Paralyzed with despair, all I could do was weep (that was when the box of Kleenex on the coffee table became convenient). I couldn't talk. I couldn't stand up to walk. I couldn't even see. I was blinded by my tears. My dad, with tears streaming from his eyes, leaned over to hold me. All he could say repeatedly was, "I'm so sorry." It was just too much to process. How could this be happening? That was a legitimate out-of-body experience for me. In hindsight, I can see God's grace in that moment. I desperately needed my father to be with me, and God graced me with him exactly when I needed him.

After the original download of information, another physician asked if I had any questions. I thought, "Are you kidding me?" Of course I didn't have any questions. I couldn't think clearly enough to form one. I didn't have to say a word, though. The expression on my face clearly conveyed what was going through my mind. After what seemed like an eternity of crying (and nearly hyperventilating) while a bunch of people in white coats were staring at me, I managed as best I could to squeak the words, "I want to be alone," out of my mouth. Everyone left - including my dad. Poor thing, he just wanted to fix it for me. I still remember the look on his face as he walked out. He looked back at me as if he could save me from my pain. Daddy's little girl. But this time, there was nothing Daddy could do. Similarly, there seemed to be not much more the doctors could do. Alone in the room that had instantly become hell, I began to question God out loud with selfish conviction: "Why me? Why my child? Why any child, for that matter? What did I do that was so wrong?" My questions turned into demands. I'm not sure if one would call it a prayer, but it went a little like this:

"God, I don't understand what is going on, but I've heard what the doctors have to say. Now I want to know what you have to say. You created her. Her life has a purpose just like everyone else. This is beyond my control. YOU FIX IT."

At that moment, my daughter's condition became a spiritual battle for me. Come what may and fearful or not, I had to stand firm in my faith and on God's promises for my daughter as I walked the journey out. My confident conclusion was that Ashlyn was either going to go home to be with the Lord, or she was leaving that hospital to go home with us. Either way, I would be victorious. I truly believed that what the devil intended for harm, God would turn around for good. I was convinced that somehow this unthinkable scenario was going to bring about some good.

Although I was still in utter shock from the clinical overload, I managed to pull myself together and walk out of "the room," trusting that God was in total control. From that point on, over the course of another three months, I simply took one day at a time - with hope and faith functioning as my best friends.

We were very blessed to have the financial resources to fly family members in who helped and supported us. It meant so much to me, especially given how much Robert was traveling with the Rockets. Robert, Sr., a retired Army veteran, often made himself available. Lelia even considered retiring and moving to Houston. When she offered, I realized how much of an impact little Miss Ashlyn had on all our lives.

Robert would usually make his hospital visits after the team's morning practices - and sometimes again at night - but he wouldn't typically visit on game nights as they usually ended late in the evening. He was a man of very few words during that time. All the emotion and aggression he exhibited on the court was not often visible in his personal life. I have wondered over the years how Ashlyn's medical situation was affecting him mentally and emotionally. I've wondered if what he was feeling and thinking was similar to my feelings and thoughts. He never opened up, and I never pressed him. He got up every morning, went to work (i.e. practice) and was always on time. No matter what was going on in our personal lives, he didn't miss a beat. He never complained, at least not that I could hear. I had a tremendous amount of respect for him. There was so much to process as new parents, and I now know that we both experienced our own silent, private pain.

As the days and months went by, Ashlyn seemed to make drastic improvements in some areas. These improvements yielded talk of her coming home. I thought it was odd she would be released directly from NICU without first transitioning to a recovery room first, but we had been there for what seemed like forever, so I was not complaining. I wanted nothing more than to take my child home for the first time. She had been breathing on her own since the tracheostomy. She was also receiving her daily calories through the G-button without any difficulty. The goal now was for her to go home without the trachea apparatus. The plan was to remove the trachea apparatus - and if Ashlyn was breathing on her own without any respiratory aid - she would be released to go home within a two-to-three week period.

I was overcome with joy. The anticipation of that day (which was six months in the making) was becoming a reality. Robert and I were finally able to take our daughter home.

Two weeks passed and Ashlyn held her own. She was doing so well. I think the doctor was even surprised at how well she was breathing on her own. Ashlyn had proven herself a fighter. The doctor assigned her three more days in the hospital. It was such a relief to get through that initial challenge so we could move forward and get Ashlyn the therapy she needed so she could have a better quality of life. It was countdown-to-release time.

Day one passed without incident. Day two passed without incident. Day three…

Robert and I were awakened at 6:00 A.M. by the phone. I jumped up with excitement. Surely this call was to let us know what time we could expect to sign discharge papers for Ashlyn's release and walk out of that hospital for good. I answered the call. "Hello!" The doctor on the other end said, "Ashlyn had a severe setback at around 4:00 A.M. while she was sleeping. She received an emergency bedside intubation, and she is on a relatively high percentage of oxygen because of the trauma. She is sedated and resting well, but I'd like to speak with you in detail about another plan of action." I weakly replied, "We're on our way."

The phone slid from my ear onto the floor. Robert just looked at me as I sobbed. I couldn't repeat what I'd just heard, but he knew what I'd heard wasn't good news. He grabbed me and held me, not saying a word.

We quickly got dressed and headed to the hospital. When we entered the NICU, it felt like déjà vu. I walked over to Ashlyn and saw that she had been intubated... again. White surgical tape covered half of her face to support the positioning of the tube. The nurse told us that the doctor had been paged and that she would be there to talk to us right away. As we waited, I kept looking at Ashlyn. She looked exhausted, but peaceful. My heart ached to look at her in that hospital bed. But that didn't keep me from talking to her, singing to her and giving her security. Mommy was there.

The doctor got there quickly. She took us aside and expressed how deeply sorry she was that we were so close to getting Ashlyn home, but that, over the course of the night, Ashlyn's epiglottis had failed her again. It had collapsed and completely shut off her airway. She explained that her concern was the possibility of this happening when Ashlyn was at home. That wasn't something I even wanted to think about, but I knew she was right. She told us she did not feel comfortable sending Ashlyn home with a "lazy" epiglottis - with or without the trachea apparatus in place to support her airway. She asked us to think about the option of removing her epiglottis completely to avoid another episode like the one Ashlyn had just experienced. Now just so you know, there is no *Epiglottis Fairy* who leaves coins under pillows in anticipation of the growth of a new epiglottis. Once the epiglottis is gone, it is gone. For us, this option was a "no brainer." We agreed to the surgery. Within the next couple of days, the surgery was performed. The worst-case scenario for us was that Ashlyn wouldn't eat by mouth, or that if she did, she would only be able to eat minimally. Thankfully, the resolution for that issue was already in place: the G-button.

According to the Mayo Clinic's *Complete Book of Pregnancy & Baby's First Year*, a baby between four and six months old is usually playing with their fingers and toes, putting objects in their mouths and rolling over. Closer to six months of age, they are usually working hard at sitting and preparing for the introduction to solid foods. Ashlyn was nearly six months old. While recuperating from the emergency intubation, she was lying motionless in the hospital bed. She wasn't playing with her fingers and toes or bringing any objects to her mouth. She wasn't rolling over. Instead, a nurse or I would have to shift her from one side to the other so she wouldn't develop bedsores, and position rolled up baby blankets to keep her in place. Tube feedings consisting of lactose-free baby formula took the place of exploring new tastes, temperatures and textures of solid foods. Ashlyn just lay in her bed with over half of her head shaved, and a tube protruding from her mouth.

Although Robert and I were managing heavy off-the-court issues, he went on to win his first NBA Championship with the Houston Rockets against the New York Knicks. It was an exciting time for him and for the city of Houston. I went to the game and shared in the excitement, but as soon as we could, we left the arena and headed to the hospital to see Ashlyn. It seemed as if everyone in the city watched the championship game. When we got to the hospital, Robert was greeted with one shout of "Congratulations!" after another. Once we were behind the NICU doors, the cheers were replaced with the alarming sounds of beeping heart and blood pressure monitors. The visit was brief that night, but it was long enough for a good dose of humility.

The end of that particular hospital journey was near. When Ashlyn was able to get off the oxygen and breathe on her own, we knew that she was on her way to recovery, but this time in the comforts of our home.

CHAPTER FIVE

GLAMOROUS HOMECOMING

"The human capacity to fight back will always astonish doctors and philosophers. It seems, indeed, that there are no circumstances so bad and no obstacles so big that man cannot conquer them."
~Jean Tetreau

On September 29, 1994, Ashlyn was discharged from Texas Children's Hospital. Two and one-half months after receiving the dreadful news, Robert and I brought our daughter home for the first time. It was indeed a glorious day. I was excited and nervous. We had so much to bring home.

For instance, she had a chest of drawers full of clothes. That's right, clothes. Ashlyn had developed a reputation, as sick as she was, as being the best-dressed baby in NICU. I figured her being sick didn't mean she had to look sick. Included with all the pretty clothes were discharge papers (stating that her prognosis was very poor), all of her meds, medical equipment, medical supplies and the written orders for her around-the-clock nurses. Ashlyn's nursery at home was quickly transformed into her personalized hospital room. The nurses worked 24-hour shifts at our home. They were contracted at that time through a company called The Care Group, Inc. in Houston. Ashlyn was still in an extremely delicate state. Someone had to be with her at all times in the event her airway became compromised (especially during her sleep), or if her oxygen levels got too low. Having nurses around-the-clock lasted for eight months. We soon learned that the insurance company intended to reduce the nursing hours for which they would pay. I was furious. I didn't understand how anyone could make judgment calls without knowing the situation. I felt they could have at least sent someone to my home to assess the situation and properly identify Ashlyn's needs. I fought as hard as I could to maintain the nurses' hours. The insurance company agreed to slowly wean the hours, increasing them only as needed. Eventually, as Ashlyn got a bit stronger and healthier, we reduced the nursing hours to eight hours a day, seven days a week. In short, she had a night nurse. That way, I was able to rest so I could take care of her during the day.

Ashlyn began physical and occupational therapy almost immediately at our home through a program called Project Grow. I was overwhelmed once again. It went from being Robert (sometimes) and me in our home, to having a revolving door of people day and night. There were therapists, nurses, nursing supervisors and case managers. By my choice, the in-home therapy lasted just a few months. Although, I knew Ashlyn needed these services, I felt my home had been invaded. It was absolute chaos. After everything Ashlyn, Robert and I had been through, it wasn't a good feeling. I needed to explore other available options. There was not a problem with the therapists in and of themselves, I just chose to start a process of elimination.

As it turned out, other options were indeed available. On March 24, 1995, at eleven months old, Ashlyn began physical therapy, occupational therapy and speech therapy at Pediatric Therapy Center (PTC) in Houston. This was a victory because doctors said she would never to walk or talk, but we wanted to do everything we could as parents to give our daughter what she needed.

Robert and I went to her first visit together. Overtaken by the complexity of the situation, I stood quiet and withdrawn. I didn't know how to process any of it, but I was clear that I had been chosen for this task, and I was committed for the long haul.

Robert and I met a woman that same day in the lobby of the therapy center. She introduced herself and offered a rundown about why she loved the facility and all of the therapists there. She told us she had a son who had been receiving therapy for a few years. My initial feeling was terror. I was already saturated with emotions and trying to hold them all in. She was friendly, forthcoming and enthusiastic about PTC. I stood there and appeared to be quietly listening. I appreciated the encouraging feedback, but I was simply not mentally or emotionally healed enough to share her vigor.

I took Ashlyn to her next therapy visit alone. As I was signing Ashlyn in, the receptionist advised me that someone had left something for me. I didn't know anyone there except Ashlyn's three therapists, so I was more than curious about who had left something for me. She handed me an envelope. It was a very feminine floral stationery envelope with "Keva" handwritten on the front. It appeared to be harmlessly intended, so I read it.

[*sic*]

Keva,

First of all it was a great pleasure to meet you, Robert and Ashlyn at PTC on Friday. I'm sorry that you missed your appointment but I can not tell you how many times I've done that and we don't live that close.

I'm writing you this note to let you know you've got a friend and someone to talk to that understands if you ever need that. When I was 23 we had our first son, Bobby. When I was 26 we had Tony, 10 weeks early and he was very unhealthy. Within six months Bobby was diagnosed with Williams Syndrome (missing 7q chromosome) and Tony with Cerebral Palsy.

Needless to say, my life has taken a very different path than I had planned. Doctors, hospitals, medicines, therapists, surgeries and worst of all, not many people have any idea what I go through on a daily basis. Sometimes I even wonder if my husband does. He's very helpful and a wonderful father but I often envy the fact that he gets to take off to work each day and "sort of" forget our troubles at home. He swears he never does. It's been very difficult for me not to be jealous of my friends' children and my 9 nieces and nephews. When they are discussing walking at 9 months, talking at 1 year, feeding themselves and now riding bicycles it is so foreign to me. I only wish and pray for these to come true for my children at any age. Don't get me wrong, I adore my children and I feel like the Lord chose me to be the caregiver and mother, but all the therapies, etc. can really get you down.

My family is in California. They are very supportive and helpful when they can be but I really rely on my friends here in Houston. We've lived here for 4 years now. Houston has so much to offer in the way of medical needs, so I'm actually grateful to be here for the children. And by the way, Beverly is a fantastic Physical Therapist. We've been to many and she is far and above "the best." Tony had major back surgery by a world renown Neuro Surgeon in California at U.C.L.A. His name is Warwick Peacock. He's not only brilliant, but

*a super nice man. He recommends Beverly highly. The
whole center is very professional and you can trust them
completely. We've been going there for 4 years (both
boys) and have never had 1 complaint.
I'm wondering how you've handled all that's been
dealt to you, you look so calm and a real natural at
motherhood. Robert too! You both are so lucky to have
Ashlyn and each other. Try to remember to always have
some time away with each other. We figured this out
almost too late but it's so important to go out on dates
and enjoy each other and everything you've been blessed
with. Call me any time you need to.*

~Gilly A.

After reading the letter, I cried and cried. I cried for
Gilly and me. I was emotional for her because she had
gone through so much, yet she selflessly reached out to me
- a total stranger - to give me hope, but to also let me know
the reality of our situation. At the time I couldn't relate to
everything she'd written. I'm not sure my brain had the
capacity to see beyond what was physically in front of
me. The ability to see the big picture as she had written
it was almost inconceivable. I was twenty-three years
old and everything was happening at once dizzyingly
quickly and achingly slowly.

Somehow, I convinced myself that what Gilly described
in her letter was *her* life and that my life was going to be
different. Very different. I appreciated her sharing her story
and my heart went out to her, but I was convinced that Ashlyn
was going to be just fine. I reasoned, "What's a few months of
therapy? We can do this. This is temporary. I have faith that

God will fix it. After that, she'll be walking and talking and she will be 'normal'." Denial? Maybe. Hopeful? Definitely.

We all want our perfect worlds. Although I appreciated what Gilly shared with me, I was not ready to receive it until much later. When I was ready to receive it, the hope, wisdom and understanding came with ease. I didn't realize at the time that Gilly's letter was, in many ways, prophetic. As time passed, I saw how our lives paralleled.

Ashlyn and I went to therapy three-to-four days a week. We had the same routine every day. PTC became our second home. After a while, Ashlyn began to dislike it. It was getting old for me, too. When she was two years old (but physically looking twelve months old), a new phase of her behavior manifested. I noticed when I would pull into the therapy parking lot, she would cry a silent, angry cry because she recognized where we were and what was about to happen. I marveled at her awareness. My heart broke every time I took her out of her car seat. She cried so hard, but there was no sound. Imagine that. Without sound, the translation of her cry was "I don't want to be here!"

Despite feeling helpless and grief-stricken as I watched her reaction, I knew therapy was the best thing for her. We pushed through it each time. I don't know for which one of us it was harder. Most times I would sit in on her sessions, but sometimes I opted to sit in the lobby for some brief alone time.

Although Robert had a basketball off-season, taking Ashlyn to her therapy appointments, doctor appointments and her day-to-day care was my year-round responsibility. That just became the dynamic in our home. There was no right or wrong where that was concerned. It just happened that way. No matter how mentally, emotionally and physically overwhelming things got for me, somehow it just didn't feel right to complain. I was Ashlyn's primary caregiver, and that was the way things remained.

I observed other mom's bringing their children in for therapy. I heard conversations some of them had with each other. Some of them knitted. Some of them read. Others talked on the phone. They needed alone time, too. I noticed a common need among us: the need for adult company and conversations. We shared a need to exhale. That lobby became our source of temporary stillness from the emotional stresses of caring for special-needs children. I wondered if that was my new sorority. There are secrets and stories that only one caregiver of a child with special-needs can share with another. There are no secret handshakes, however there is an unspoken specific requirement of this special group of men and women - unwavering dedication and commitment. During this time, I felt like an outsider within my new care-giving family. Although I did communicate with some of the mom's, I did not reveal to anyone that I was engaged to rising NBA star Robert Horry. I also did not reveal that Ashlyn was his daughter. I was not ashamed of Ashlyn or the fact that Robert was her father. I didn't reveal the information because I didn't believe it was necessary to introduce the world of celebrity to the world of Ashlyn's physical care.

I was especially adamant about it since both worlds were new to me, and I often felt isolated. It was extremely difficult for me to process everything going on medically with Ashlyn. I didn't understand it, but I was trying. Basketball, big arenas, fame and money presented an entirely different dynamic to process. Ironically, it was at that time (in 1995) that Robert and the Rockets were blessed to win a second NBA Championship. Once again the city of Houston was charged with an indescribable energy. It was amazing. I was happy for him and how his career was taking off, but still uncertain about what was actually happening within that realm of success, and the magnitude of it.

I'm a relatively private person. I wasn't used to the attention a person's name could bring. I steered myself away from that attention at all costs, and focused on our daughter's health. It was like living a double life, and like living in two totally different worlds. It took awhile before I allowed the two worlds to converge. I had even asked Robert not to share information on Ashlyn or about our family to the media until we knew for certain that Ashlyn was out of the woods and until we knew more about her condition. He agreed. That's how it was for several years.

Since the day Ashlyn was born Robert and I have never talked about his feelings regarding her situation, and how it affected him. I always shared, whether he asked me to or not. I expressed my frustrations, my joys and of course, I yelled from the mountaintop the excitement I felt when Ashlyn reached every milestone. Robert listened, but he never shared his feelings. Ashlyn's health challenges had to be just as difficult for him (if not more in some ways) as it was for me. Regardless of our one-sided communication, I'm grateful he lent me his ear, as it helped me to process my pain along the way.

~THE FIRST MEDICAL REVELATION~

In August 1995, Robert and I received a letter from the Department of Molecular and Human Genetics at Baylor College of Medicine. The letter served as a formal recording of some of the information related to Ashlyn's chromosome abnormality. It explained that Ashlyn had a number of birth defects, all of which were caused by an abnormality in her chromosome #1. The birth defects included a delay in her development and learning, the severe Laryngomalacia, the renal tubular acidosis and the difficulty in feeding and growth. All of these problems resulted from the piece of one of the chromosome #1 that was missing. In the letter, the geneticists were calling the abnormality "an interstitial deletion of the short arm of chromosome #1." The letter further explained that because of the condition's rarity, no specific predictions could be made regarding the severity of her problems. The letter also gave a detailed explanation about chromosomes, saying they are the physical packages inside every cell in the body - which is where genes live. Humans have forty-six chromosomes, and they exist in twenty-three pairs. The first twenty-two chromosome pairs are called *autosomes*, and they are numbered based on their size. Chromosome #1 is the largest of the human chromosomes. Because of the deleted region in Ashlyn's chromosome #1, there were probably hundreds - or even a thousand or more - genes missing from one of the chromosome #1. Therefore, a large number of genes were out of balance.

While Robert and I appreciated receiving the letter – and the attempt at an explanation about what was happening with Ashlyn – we found no solace in the new information. We also found no definitive answers. All we knew was that our daughter was ill and no one seemed to know exactly what was wrong with her, or how to fix it.

~HERE COMES THE BRIDE~

After some time, things had finally calmed down enough for Robert and I to breathe a little. With no prognosis in sight, but with Ashlyn at home, we decided to get married in Houston. Aside from the day I gave birth to our daughter, it was the best day of my life. It was my day. I wasn't the typical nervous bride. I don't think I had one butterfly in my stomach. I owned that day. There was no turning back at that point. After saying our vows before God, our family and friends, I felt that my family was complete. My fiancé was now my husband. I felt a spiritual sigh of relief. Our plans as a couple were lived out.

Our whole family, as well as close friends, had flown to Houston for our special occasion. We had four hundred guests. Until that day, I didn't realize we even knew four hundred people. It felt good to have Ashlyn take part in such a joyous occasion. Her pearl-adorned ivory silk dress flowed as she was carried down the aisle of the church to the traditional bridal march. She was absolutely beautiful. Ashlyn didn't have a clue about what was going on, but all of the guests stood for her as she complemented my grand entrance. My father walked me down the aisle to

Whitney Houston's "I Believe in You and Me," and gave me away to my college sweetheart, the love of my life and the father of my first-born child. I didn't feel differently, but I was more than aware that on that day we were officially pronounced *"Mr. & Mrs. Robert Horry."*

I was hopeful.

~ SCHOOL~

When Ashlyn started school, there were many different things that I was faced with for the first time, including Admission, Review and Dismissal (ARD) meetings, which were usually held to review all services, goals and the need for any additional help for the child. I was also introduced to Individual Education Plans (IEPs), which were the academic goals set up specifically for the child. IEP also detailed the rules and documentations that come with the schooling of a special-needs child. The thing I hated the most was having to relive every detail of Ashlyn's medical history each time a new person was integrated with her education plans. Her ARD meetings included at least eight people, sometimes more. Everyone had to be on the same page and working toward the same goals.

Her first school, Allen Parkway Elementary was in Sugar Land, Texas. This school was part of the Preschool Programs for Children with Disabilities (PPCD) program. I'm grateful for Ashlyn's teacher, Miss Elizabeth, who made her first year in school a wonderful experience. Miss Elizabeth was a young and dedicated woman who cared deeply for her "babies" (as she referred to the children she taught). She kept in touch and followed Ashlyn's progress. We were so blessed to have her as Ashlyn's first teacher. Although she helped make the transition easier, I was still an emotional wreck on her first day of school. I cried uncontrollably. Ashlyn had never been away from me. I'm sure I was no different from any other mom on their child's first day of Kindergarten, and even though the strong emotions were there, I had peace and comfort knowing Miss Elizabeth was such a kind and nurturing teacher. She caught on very quickly to the needs of each student. I knew Ashlyn was in good hands, and it was that experience that set the tone for the rest of her schooling. I was more than aware of Ashlyn's needs and to what she responded best. As her advocate, those were the things on which I had to stand firm as she has moved through the school system.

During Ashlyn's first year of school, I became pregnant with our second child. Because our first child was born with a chromosome abnormality, an amniocentesis was highly recommended. This time, we opted to get it done. I don't necessarily have a fear of needles, but I am also not exactly a fan. Robert went with me for the procedure. I was a bit uneasy and he wanted to make sure the baby wasn't accidentally stuck by the (very long) needle. We viewed the whole thing on a monitor. I was stuck twice with the needle. With each stick, the baby moved his head toward the needle. It brought tears to my eyes. It was pretty painful, and I experienced quite a bit of discomfort following the test. I had to go home and get off my feet. The hardest part of having an amniocentesis is the stressful wait for the results. By the grace of God, the results were perfect.

On February 5, 1999, God blessed us again with a beautiful baby boy, Robert Camron Horry (we call him Camron). He weighed 8 pounds, 11 ounces and was 22 ½ inches long. I knew he was a healthy baby. I was thrilled beyond description. The NBA had just ended a lockout, so no games had been played for the first half of the regular season. Robert was there for Camron's birth from start to finish. Ironically though, the first game after the lockout fell on the same evening Camron was born. Once again, the Los Angeles Lakers were playing the Houston Rockets in Los Angeles - just as they had in 1994 when Ashlyn was born. But this time, Robert was a member of the Lakers - who were playing against his former team. I was grateful he was able to be present for the birth of our son (which meant he missed his first post lockout game). It was strange. We watched the game from my hospital suite, and it warmed my heart to see Dad holding his son. Robert's being there was a sweet moment after the birth of our son. I'm glad I captured it on film because Robert had to get back to work, and he was on a plane for Los Angeles two days later. Reality set in right away. Because I didn't take Ashlyn home immediately after giving birth to her, the experience of taking Camron home was sure to be different. I was frightened - again. What was I going to do with this little person? It was at that moment, I realized God had a sense of humor (but it wasn't funny to me). Ashlyn was five years old. As badly as I wanted a second child, I kind of forgot to factor in two things. One, I had to immediately take Camron home. Two, he was a boy. I only knew about girl stuff! A quick prayer was in order. "God help me! I have no clue about what to do here." Despite my concerns, I adapted pretty well.

CHAPTER SIX

Glamorous Character

*"A journey of a thousand miles must
begin with a single step."*
~Lao Tzu

The kids were five years apart. I knew Camron would have limited interaction with Ashlyn; not because of the age difference, but because of her different abilities. But love endures all and conquers all. Ashlyn loved her baby brother immeasurably. She would pull up to a standing position next to his playpen or his crib and marvel as she stared at him. She was so happy with him. She may have thought him to be a play toy.

As Camron got older, Ashlyn didn't let it bother her. She was still "the big sister in charge." She loved him even more. They developed their own language with each other. They had their own way of communicating. When Ashlyn would play too rough with Camron, grabbing at his legs as he walked by bringing him down to her level on the floor, (or putting him in a headlock) he didn't complain. He didn't even cry. He figured out his own method of dealing with his sister and learning her ways that was privately between them.

Against everything doctors told us, and every odd we were told couldn't be defied, Ashlyn began walking at about age seven. It actually started as a game Robert and I played with her. I would prop her up with her back against the billiard table in our game room so she would feel secure. Robert would stand about five feet away (my feet, not his size fifteen's) and coax her to take steps toward him. He would sometimes use a toy or a book;

whatever object would gain her attention. The first few times nothing happened, but eventually she caught on. She would gingerly take a step or two, and literally fall forward with confidence that one of us would catch her. After a while, she really got the hang of it. Each time we practiced, she would take more steps. She was still unstable and unsure, but it was a major achievement for her to move from one point to another.

Since Ashlyn was making such great strides (figuratively and literally) her physical therapist suggested she get a walker to aid in her mobility. Her walker was called a gate walker. It was sometimes incorporated in her physical therapy sessions. She would access it from the rear, and we would position her into a Velcro harness that fastened around her torso as tightly or as loosely as she needed it (depending on her stamina). This helped her feel secure as she explored new territory. If she wanted out, someone would have to physically take her out. She could not get in and out independently. Not only did it offer Ashlyn aid in mobility, it helped her learn to place pressure on her feet for different increments of time. She was primarily accustomed to lying down or being propped up, pushed in a stroller or carried. The walker was a sure way of allowing Ashlyn's ankles, legs and hips to get stronger over time, and for her to gain confidence in the mechanism of walking.

Ashlyn began the new school year with her gate walker. She had a difficult time navigating through that particular school. The halls were outside, and the walking surface was cemented rocks and gravel. It didn't qualify as a safe environment for Ashlyn or others when she was in the walker. I was concerned for her safety - as well as for the safety of the other kids - in the event she had an accident in the walker.

I remember having an ARD meeting that year, and the physical therapist appointed through the school district to work with Ashlyn recommended - with at least ten other people in the meeting - that I put Ashlyn in a wheelchair. She had already worked with Ashlyn for a few months by that time. As the person who knew how far Ashlyn had come with physical mobility, the thought of keeping her confined did not sit well with me. The only vision I would allow myself to see was one of Ashlyn walking without a walker or any assistance. To confine her to a wheelchair when she was plainly showing determination to walk was totally defeating the purpose. Needless to say, I never took into consideration the suggestion the physical therapist offered. In my mind, the objective (and one of Ashlyn's specific educational goals) was to be as independent as possible, and to function as normally as her body would allow. Ashlyn's willingness and determination to walk was in and of itself a victory. I wasn't about to take that away from her. I let her take the lead. As a group, we all came to an agreement on a schedule as to when Ashlyn would take to the halls with her walker (while avoiding running over the other kids). It was a joy to watch her working so hard walking the halls of her school and trying her best to interact with the other students.

Not long after that, Ashlyn had a significant growth spurt and her strength began to increase. So much so in fact, she began picking up the walker by the handgrips as she walked. She didn't do it smoothly or consistently of course, but she did it enough for us to know we needed to make a change. Her private physical therapist was consistently working with her on walking and strengthening her core. Gaining strength and flexibility in her calves and hip flexors was extremely important because Ashlyn was quite stiff. Her range of motion was limited. At that point, her physical therapist suggested a different walker. The one she suggested allowed Ashlyn access from the front and it had no trunk support. It was also lightweight. She could access it independently and easily. That was an easy choice for us. Ashlyn got comfortable with the new walker in no time, and she chose an airport, of all places, to demonstrate her new skills.

We had just gotten through security at George Bush Intercontinental airport in Houston. Ashlyn had her new walker and I was carrying Camron (in a kangaroo pouch), his diaper bag and all of Ashlyn's equipment. I was listening for the clanking sound of her walker as we hurried to catch our flight. We were pushing it. Boarding time was down to the wire. I was walking as quickly as I could, weighed down with everything. I was also acutely conscious of the fact that I could not get too far ahead of Ashlyn. She was working so hard to walk the long distance to the gate. Suddenly I heard someone say, "Ma'am! Ma'am!" I turned to see if the person was addressing me. I didn't hear the clanking noise anymore. It seemed to be a distant bell among all the commotion.

What I saw astonished me.

Ashlyn had completely walked out of her walker, left it behind and was walking on her own. "Oh my gosh!" I yelled (scaring Camron). What was I supposed to do with this one? I was so blown away, I could've been sold for half a penny. What a happy dilemma. On one hand, I was so excited I wanted to drop everything, scream, cry with joy and take it all in. I was beyond proud of her. On the other hand, I wanted to scream in frustration because I knew we were going to miss our flight. I thought to myself, "Ashlyn...now? In the airport? Of all times, why now?" The giant grin on her face told me she knew she had achieved something big. As I fought to hold back tears of joy, I turned and went back as quickly as I could to get her walker. I scooped it with the one hand already carrying Ashlyn's carry-on bag and Camron's diaper bag, grabbed her hand with my free hand and bolted for our gate. We'd made it just seconds before the flight crew shut the door. We were the last people to board.

Considering the cumbersome arranging of all my belongings, I'm sure we delayed takeoff by several minutes. So there we were, California bound with Ashlyn walking. My girl. It could not have been more thrilling (and nerve-wracking). This was one of Ashlyn's finest hours. My greatest hallelujah moment happened when she started walking alone...in a crowded airport.

~RETAIL THERAPY~

NBA commentators have always commented on Robert's long arms. I'm sure that asset is wonderful to have when you are rebounding and stealing basketballs. In Ashlyn's case, she found another creative use for her inherited long limbs. She loved to demonstrate this skill in stores. I call it sideswiping. She would be looking at me or distracted by something off in the distance when suddenly, without warning, she would sideswipe an entire shelf of merchandise. Ashlyn thought it was hilarious. I didn't. In my fury, I would pick everything up and place the disheveled products back on the shelf. Many times, an employee would come over and say (pitifully), "I've got it ma'am. Don't worry about it." Early on, this behavior would embarrass me (as it would anyone). Once I realized it was one of her ways of communicating, the embarrassment stopped. I began to use those moments to teach Ashlyn *and* the rubberneckers who had forgotten they were rudely gawking. I'd look Ashlyn squarely in her eyes and talk to her in a very firm voice. The voice she knew meant, "Momma ain't playin'!" I'd say, "Ashlyn, this is not acceptable. If you are tired and want to go home, you will have to find another way to express yourself without damaging other people's things. Now, you have to pick up your mess." She would cry, but as she cried, she'd bend over to pick up one item at a time and place it on the shelf. Time consuming? You bet. Whether or not I would make her help me pick up the merchandise would depend on the situation and how much time I had to teach her the lesson. It was important for Ashlyn to learn through repetition, experience cause-and-effect and manage choices and consequences. Her challenges did not negate the fact that she had to learn life lessons. Again, the goal was for Ashlyn to be as independent as possible. I used moments like that as teaching opportunities for her - just as I would with Camron.

The fact was she would usually exhibit that behavior when she was tired. That was her way of communicating to me that she wanted to go home. I could never predict when she would communicate through sideswiping, but it eventually lessened. When it happened, I dealt with it. There were things I'd incorporate to help Ashlyn feel included, and she would be less likely to show off her stocking skills in public. I let her push the shopping cart (which she loved). I'd pull unbreakable items from the shelf and let her place them gently into the cart - which resulted in big smiles. When we'd reach the check out lane, I would allow her to help me place the items on the conveyor belt. I am always sensitive to those in line behind us, keeping in mind that not everyone has a high level of patience. But then there are those who are kind, helpful and would cheer Ashlyn on. Praise was always a good deterrent for undesirable behavior. She ate it up.

After checking out, I'd let Ashlyn push the shopping cart to the car. She would be all smiles again; not because of the task she'd been assigned, but because she'd get to experience the sensory stimulation from the cart rolling over the parking lot asphalt. It was bumpy, noisy and vibrated the handle she was holding. It was an adventure for her, and priceless for me to watch.

While Ashlyn was my sweet angel, my hard worker and my prankster, she was also my little stubborn manipulator. I say that with the utmost affection. This behavioral issue was one I hated with a passion. Not because of embarrassment, but because she could've seriously hurt herself or someone else. She would drop to the floor at any given moment when someone was walking with her. If she made up her mind that she didn't want to go, she would suddenly and dangerously drop her body to the floor. The unexpected movement could've been harmful not only to Ashlyn, but to the person caring for her. When she got bigger and stronger, I would try and entice her with things I knew she liked. I would offer her a book to read, but I'd tell her she had to get off the floor.

One time, she dropped to the ground in the parking lot at therapy. There was a car waiting for us to clear the path so they could have the right-of-way. There I was, verbally and physically pleading with her to get off of the ground so the car could pass. This time I was embarrassed and angry. I got behind Ashlyn with all of my bags falling off my shoulders, bent down and scooped her up to her feet by placing the folds of my arms under her armpits. Off we went - with me scolding her the whole way. By the time we walked into the therapist's office and sat in the waiting room, I was hot, sweaty and furious. My blood pressure had risen to boil and the Houston heat and humidity didn't help.

Sounds *glamorous*, doesn't it?

The therapist came out to get Ashlyn for her session. I regrouped and went about the rest of my day, but not without a bruised ego. Another lesson learned, though. I received loud and clear the message that, disabilities or not, all children require discipline.

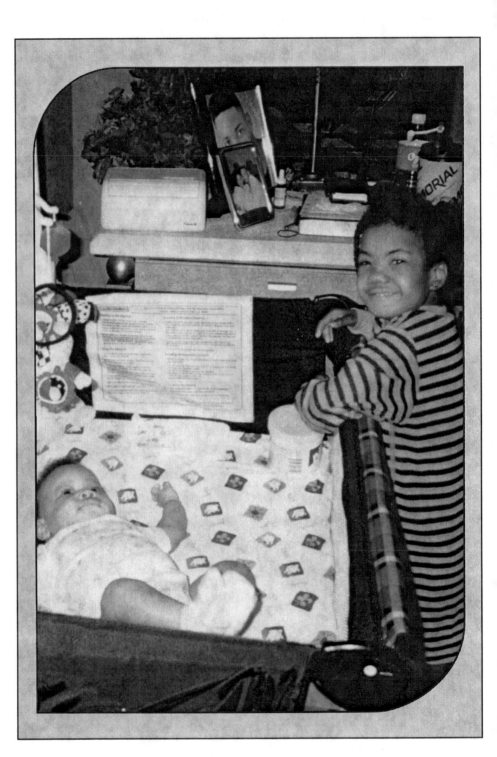

KEVA
IN
COLLEGE

ASHLYN'S
ARRIVAL

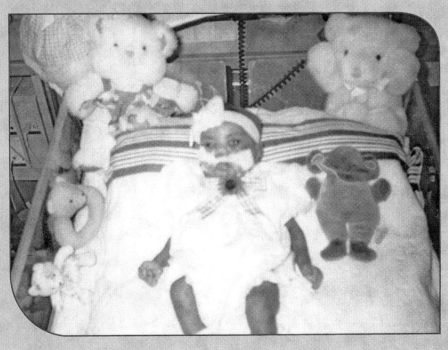

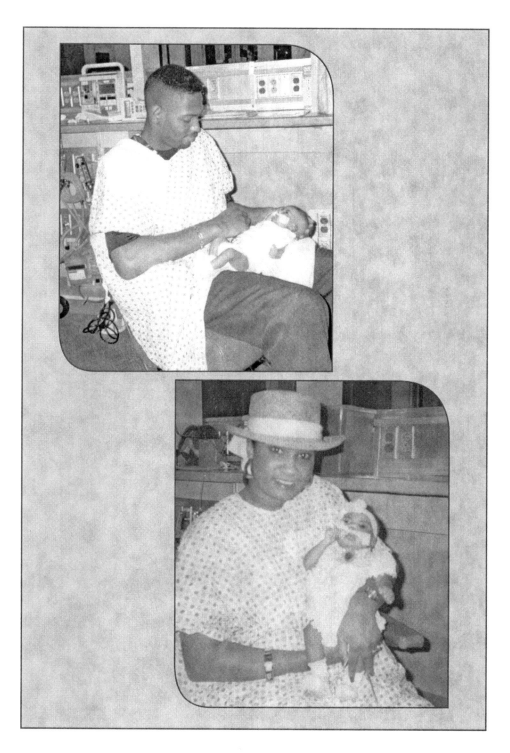

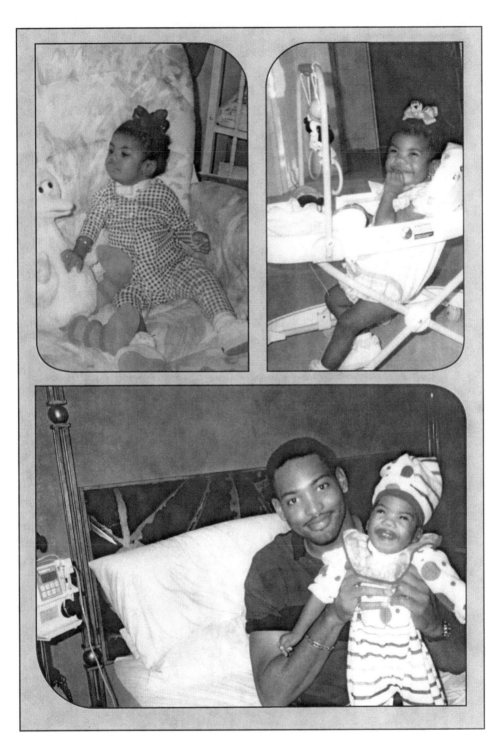

ASH
AT
SCHOOL

79

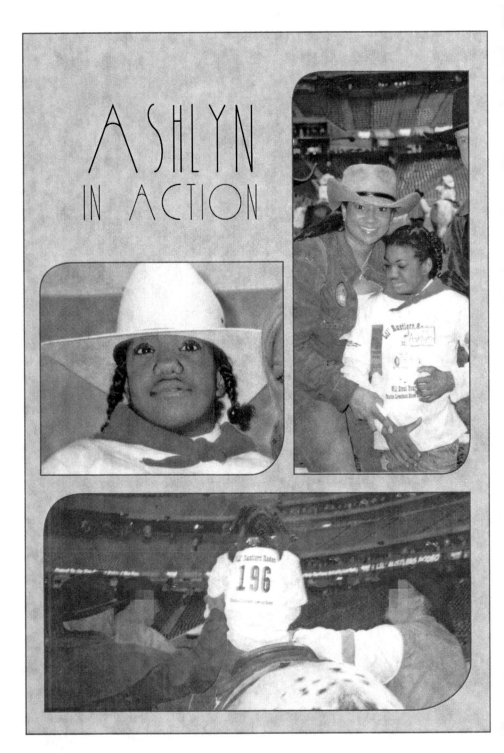

ASHLYN
IN ACTION

JUST ASH

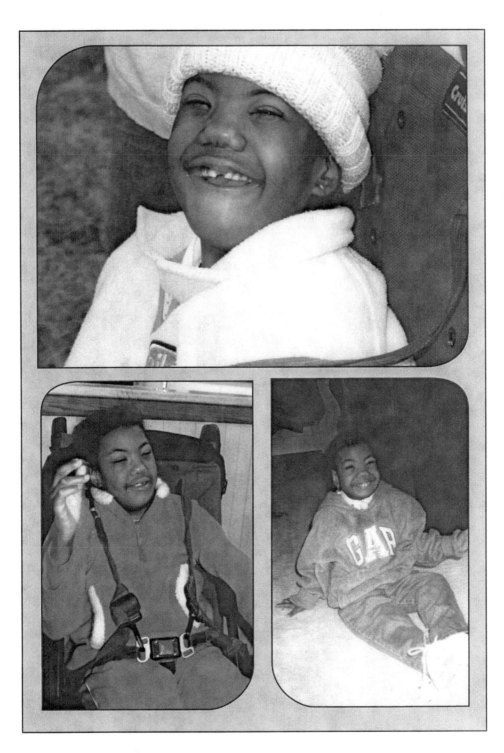

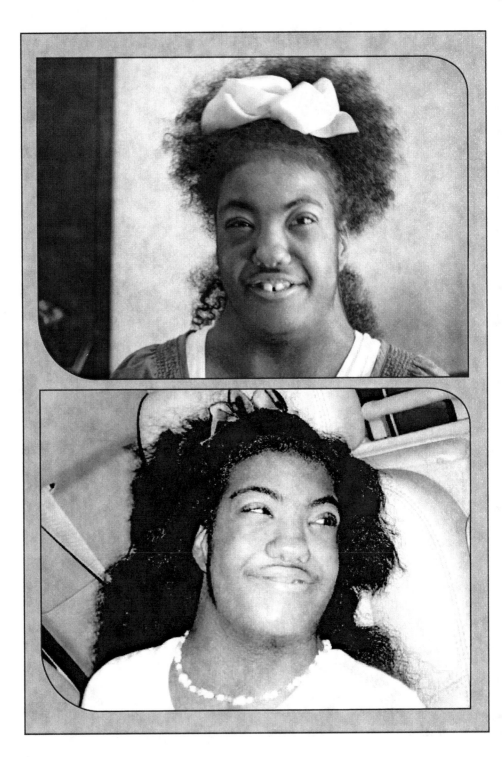

JUST CAM

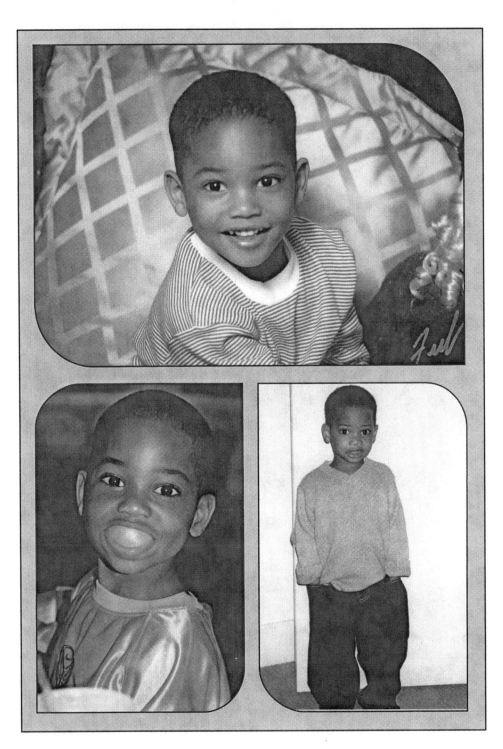

ASH AND CAM

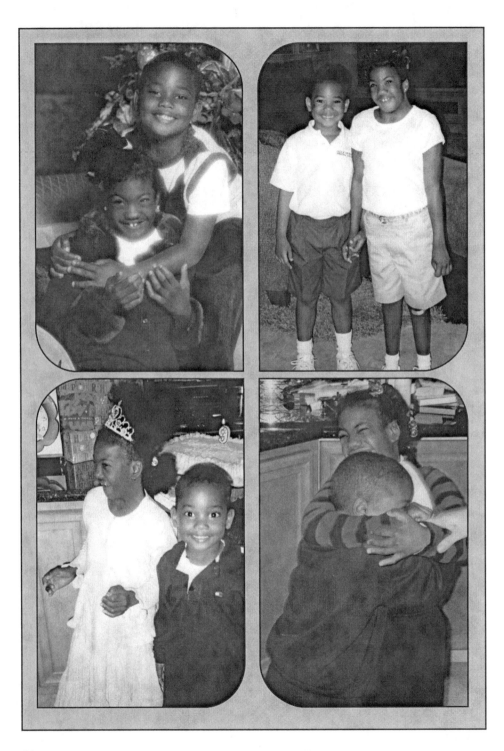

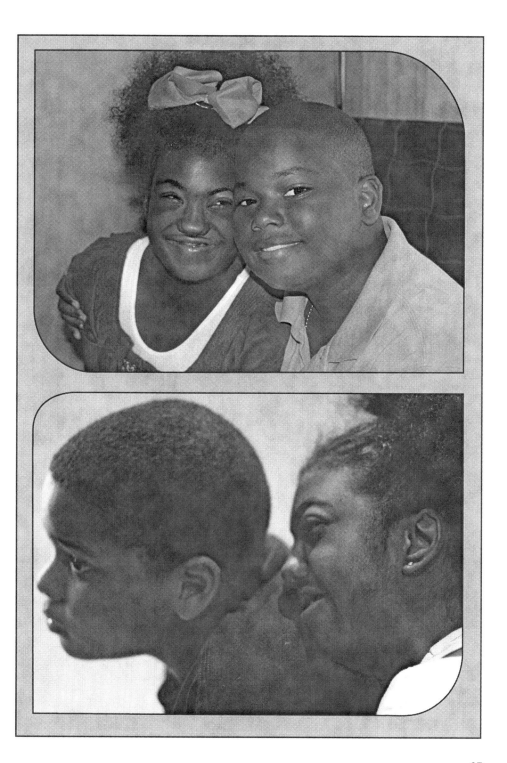

FAMILY

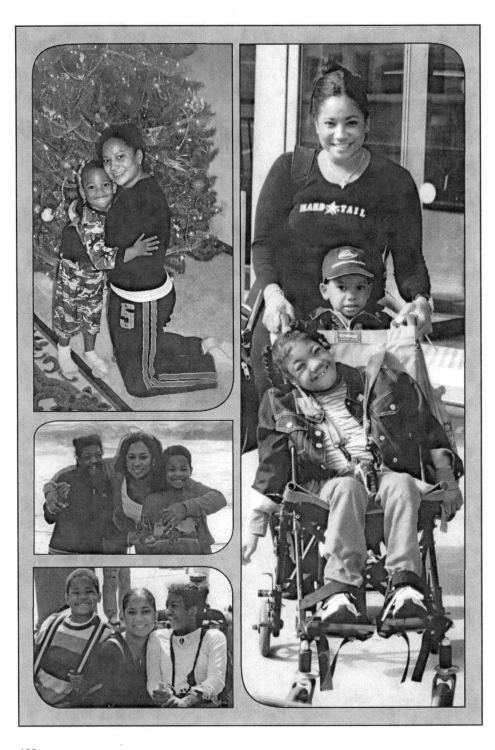

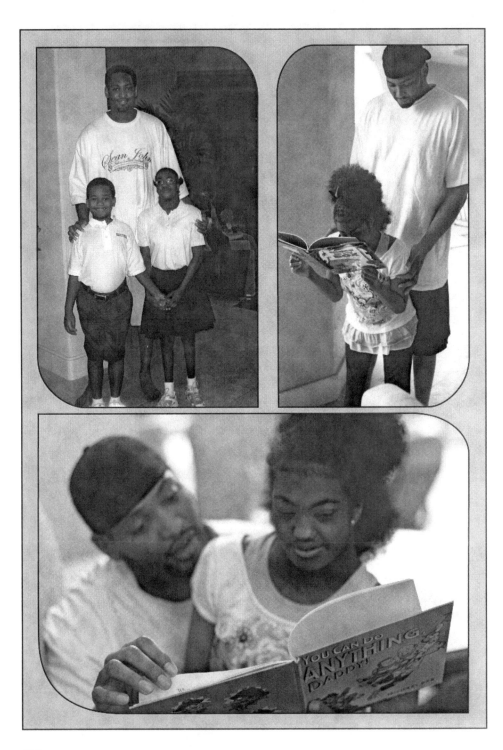

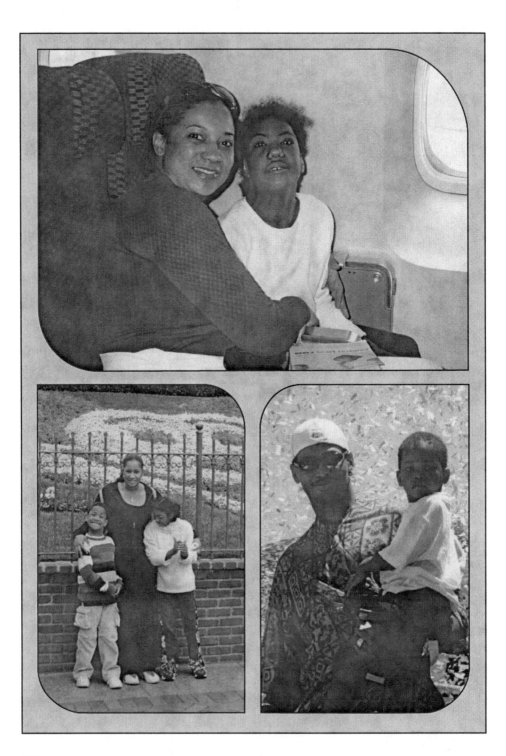

GRADUATION

Presented to

Ashlyn Horry Foundation

*In grateful appreciation for
your support of the
San Bernardino County
Superintendent of Schools*

2012
Annual Special Needs
Prom

GLAMOROUS SECLUSION

*"I was taught that the way of progress
is neither swift nor easy."*
~Marie Curie

The concepts of purpose and position seemed beyond my grasp. Here I was with four years of higher education under my belt, married to a professional athlete, caring for a child with special needs, raising another child and living a rare lifestyle that included excitement, glamour and celebrity. Maybe the difficulty I had with grasping purpose and position was a reflection of my twenty-something age. Maybe it was because I had found myself thrust into an existence that was unfathomable just a few years prior - when I was living much more simply in my quaint, grounded hometown. There were many days I asked God why I was here. I asked Him why I was going through such a trial. I asked Him about the purpose of my life. There were many days I was indescribably drained – in every conceivable way.

One day I would feel as if I was perpetually behind in life, futilely trying catch up. On another day, I would feel I was stuck in quicksand, and living without any productivity, which left me feeling paralyzed. I had been an achiever all my life. I come from a family of educators in the south. For me, that had always meant having and attaining goals. When I was growing up, my dad would always tell me I represented more than just myself. Hearing that throughout my childhood set the tone for my developing high standards for myself (and others). I was searching for direction in the throes of my wife and mommy roles. I didn't feel I was contributing to the family by solely being a stay-at-home mom. I convinced myself I could manage a career and family. "People do it all the time," I reasoned. But I quickly reality-checked myself, admitting that my circumstances were different. I had no family in Houston to rely on for help and support. I had to do what needed to be done. And, without realizing it, I had become a "married-single mom." That was not what I had envisioned my family life would be.

Over the years, I have learned the difference between acquaintances, seasonal friends and confidantes. It's a blessing to have found some confidantes in Houston (some of whom I had to depend on repeatedly for support with daily life in my husband's absence). But confidantes are few in number and, frankly, they have to be qualified. I know that sounds bold, but it's true.

As the wife of a professional athlete, trusting others was no longer easy (like it was growing up in a small town). Eventually, trusting others became a full-blown vetting process. I learned my trust couldn't be freely given - it had to be earned. I learned an unfortunate truth: not everyone was cheering for the well being of my marriage or my family. I learned some people considered my marriage a vulnerable target. I learned some people considered the fact that much of my attention was focused on Ashlyn's health as an open door to bring distraction, chaos and destruction to my marriage.

Being Robert's wife meant I had to quickly assess unfamiliar places and unfamiliar people. This reality made it difficult to make and maintain solid friendships, although I think our choice to make Houston our permanent home was a good one. Robert and I made that decision solely based on Ashlyn's medical needs, as her scenario was often a matter of life and death. But even with the little social life I did manage to establish, I always felt behind the proverbial eight ball. I couldn't keep up. I was constantly invited to social events, but was never able to attend them all because every decision was contingent on Ashlyn's health. I had the desire to nurture old friendships, meet new people and make new friends, but my every move was determined by Ashlyn. I couldn't simply ask the neighbor's daughter to babysit. Whoever cared for Ashlyn had to be specifically trained to do it properly.

I felt as if life was passing me by. I was going through the motions. I was doing what I was supposed to do as far as taking care of Ashlyn and my family, but inside I felt lifeless and lonely. The isolation was so strong at times, I was certain I had emotionally checked out. That was the hand I had been dealt, and I was convinced I had no say in the matter. "Just deal with it," I would tell myself. My "career" was caring for my daughter. I was in the most intense on-the-job-training experience I could imagine. When people asked me how I did it, I gave everyone the same response, "I don't think about it. I just do it."

No two days were ever the same. There were the days when I couldn't do anything. The monotony wore me out. I was depressed, (although I didn't realize it). I was naïve about the fact that the level of stress I experienced in my twenties had become my "normal." Of course, I didn't recognize what I was experiencing as stress. All I knew was there seemed to be a great divide between my life before Ashlyn and my life with Ashlyn. I fought and struggled in frustration with my faith; with what God's word had told me and promised me. Many people believe Christians who live faith-driven lives are somehow excluded from trials and tribulations. Actually, the exact opposite is true. Living a faith-filled life automatically draws a bull's eye on the back of the believer. This is precisely why the claim that Christianity "is for the weak" is asinine. To those people making that claim, I respectfully extend this challenge: try it. Try not doing what *you* know to do in every life situation, and instead unwaveringly obeying what God says to do. See how easy it is to deny self and submit to what appears to be the exact opposite of what will make difficulties go away. See how the definition of "weak" suddenly changes when loving the unlovable, honoring the dishonorable and biting the tongue (rather than unleashing it) increases your quality of life. Go ahead. Try it. For those who are up for the challenge, I am one hundred percent certain that the word "weak" will cease to apply to the word Christianity. The enemy is not bothered by people without faith in God - they're working on his team. It's God's warriors who unnerve the enemy. The good news is, it's faith that shields and protects us through those trials and tribulations. God's team wins this thing. It's rigged.

That being said, I often felt as if a chunk of my life was in waiting mode. I was waiting for doctors to offer more information on Ashlyn's medical condition. I was waiting to go back to school. I was waiting for the end of basketball seasons to spend quality time with my husband. I was always waiting. While waiting, I was holding out hope that one day my life would change, and that the enormous stress level would lift. I desperately wanted positive change. I wanted my family together as a unit. I wanted our daughter healthy. I was tired of wrestling with the heaviness of guilt of stealing moments away from my children to enjoy myself - sometimes just to exhale. Because I didn't know much about Ashlyn's diagnosis, my mind would stay on her even in my stolen moments. I was always on guard. Anything could happen with her at any given moment. And, it often did.

Isolation was a constant obstacle to overcome. It was usually easier to surrender to it rather than fight against it. But in the isolation came assertiveness. A visit to the park with Ashlyn was a lonely experience. I watched other moms push their kids in swings or run around chasing behind them. Despite my not being able to do those things, I somehow made myself own those moments. I got the looks and stares. No one actually questioned me about why I was talking to what appeared to be a six-month-old baby (she was two years old) in a stroller. No one asked why I would sit in a child's swing holding a baby that could barely move, and singing to her as if she were the only one in the park. I didn't care at all what others thought of me or of Ashlyn. Ashlyn enjoyed being there as much as I did. I would have loved to be chasing my daughter around and playing till she dropped, but that wasn't our reality. Being assertive in our joy when it didn't look "normal" - when everyone was staring at us - was a moment of surrender for Ashlyn and me.

Meanwhile, to my surprise, I had unknowingly formed resentment toward my husband. I had managed to keep it suppressed (which made it even more dangerous). He had basketball. He could leave home, interact with other adults and come back home. He could pursue his dreams. I couldn't. I felt trapped. I remembered Gilly's letter, and became even more connected with the parallels in our lives; the same parallels I'd said wouldn't exist when I first read her letter. I envied my husband's life. Not in terms of the celebrity, but just the fact that he had a life. He had a life, by the way, of which I was extremely proud and supportive. But I was struck by the polar opposites developing in our marriage. He was living a dream. I no longer had them. He was living his life. Life was slowly draining me. He would walk out the door and not have to deal with "our" every day reality in the way I did. All of these opposites made me feel alone. Still, even while dwelling in that place of despair, I managed to love harder and devote myself to our family with even more vigor, intensity and unyielding passion. I just wanted the discontentment to end. Life is about choices. So, I made a conscious choice, and said the following words to myself, "This is your life now. It's no longer about you. It's about our family." The internal struggle was over. I was at peace.

Or so I thought.

~THE UNEXPECTED VISITOR~

All parents dread the puberty and teenage years. There are so many challenges teenagers go through and, after having come through it with my own battle scars, I definitely would not want to do it again. I was never able to think that far ahead with Ashlyn. I just had to take each stage as it came. I wasn't even certain she would go through puberty given the limited insight about her diagnosis.

In the summer of 2005, I rented an apartment in Alabama while taking a couple courses to finish my degree. Ashlyn and Camron stayed with Lelia at her home three hours away. I drove there to spend the weekends with them.

One day, Lelia called. She said Ashlyn had started her menstrual cycle.

I was in no way prepared to hear that news. Ashlyn was just eleven. Her doctor had mentioned a few times that I should start thinking about finding an OB/GYN for her as she had already begun physically maturing. But I just didn't expect it to happen. That's the simple truth.

It was excruciating to know I wasn't there with her when she first menstruated. All I could think of was how much pain she must have been in, and the fact that she could not understand what was going on in her body. I called my OB/GYN and asked for some advice on whether to allow the cycles or to explore the option to stop them. The main reason I was interested in possibly stopping her cycles was because I was not the only one caring for her, and I didn't want to put others in the position of managing such a task. I'm sensitive to the truth that, quite likely, no one but me would care for Ashlyn during her time of the month the way I would. I didn't want to take the chance. It was difficult enough that she was wearing Pull-Ups® every day, and had to be cleaned by others when I wasn't there. Adding a menstrual cycle to that equation was a bit much for her other caregivers to take on. I didn't want anyone other than me managing it.

Nevertheless, I wanted all the information I could get regarding our options. My doctor explained that I could allow nature to take its course and let her have a cycle every month. Or, I could put her on birth control. Or, we could go to the extreme and she could have a hysterectomy...at eleven years old. The only option that made sense to me was to let nature take its course. That choice meant a lot more work and even more demand on me, but I wanted Ashlyn to have as normal an existence as possible. Menstrual cycles are part of every woman's life. There were so many "normal" things Ashlyn could not experience, and I didn't want to rob her of one more. I'm not a masochist or a martyr. I just didn't want to interrupt what was right with her body. I know many may question my choice. To those who do, I pray they never have that choice to make. There's no manual for raising a child with 1p36 Deletion Syndrome.

~MELTDOWN~

On the heels of making the adjustment to Ashlyn's latest transition, in April of 2006, I lost my teacher, my protector, my cheerleader, my friend...the person who was by my side when the doctors told me Ashlyn wouldn't live. My father passed away back home in Tuscaloosa. Suddenly, the importance of my mental, emotional and physical health for Ashlyn's sake became painfully evident. I couldn't do anything. I had never imagined what it would feel like to lose a parent. After the passing of my father, my mother put her life on hold for two and one-half years to come do for me what I couldn't do for myself. She willingly, lovingly took on my role of taking care of my two children. She also continued in her role as my mom and took care of me. I was as broken, crushed and devastated as I had ever been. Little did I know, I was exactly where God needed me to be; I was clay in His hands.

No one understood the season I was in: the season of severe weakness. Robert didn't understand. My family didn't understand. My friends didn't understand. I didn't even understand. And for that reason, I humbly bowed down to the Almighty and began my restoration process. I surrendered to His sovereignty and to His everlasting grace, mercy, love and serenity. I poured my heart out to Christ in prayer, in worship and in song. I buried myself in his word. I held onto His word for dear life. The Promise that says I "shall mount up with wings as an eagle and soar" got me through my agony. My mom being there gave me a chance to rest, recharge and prepare to fight back.

After a couple of months I began to take baby steps toward my healing. I sought counseling and spiritual guidance from my pastor and his wife. I kept my eyes, mind and heart stayed on my Bible - feeding myself spiritually. I started exercising again and before I knew it, I began to get very serious about finishing school. Getting my degree was unfinished business. Focusing on things that made me happy helped me greatly. These were small steps, but I was inching my way back to where I belonged. As time passed, the pain lessened. I began to reflect on the memories of my father with joy and gratitude. I love my father dearly and miss him very much, but I have come to understand that death brings about birthing experiences. My life was starting to shift. I was in transition.

~BIG LITTLE BROTHER~

On September 27, 2007 - at thirteen years old - Ashlyn went into the hospital with pneumonia. This was her second battle with it in her lifetime. At that point, Robert was playing for the San Antonio Spurs - his fourth NBA team.

That stay in the hospital brought a new change in our family dynamic. The first week Ashlyn spent in the hospital I felt it was important for Camron (who was eight years old) to see her frequently. It was important for both of them. For Ashlyn, I thought it would make her feel better. She loved her brother. When he walked in her hospital room, she smiled from ear to ear, oxygen mask and all. The visits served Camron well, too. He needed to be with his family - not the babysitter. I tried as much as possible to maintain some sort of familiarity for both of them. Notice I didn't say normalcy. I knew it wasn't "normal" for any of us to be in the hospital - as patients or visitors - but I knew it was best for all of us to be together. There is strength in family unity.

One week later, Ashlyn was transferred to Pediatric Intensive Care Unit (PICU). It happened unexpectedly. On that morning, I had just taken Camron to school and received a phone call within minutes after I dropped him off. It was my mother, who was at the hospital with Ashlyn. "They are moving Ashlyn to PICU. She is having a difficult time breathing," she said. My heart sank to my feet. Again.

I tried to concentrate on driving and keeping my composure. I didn't want to have or cause an accident. Although I was usually able to keep them at bay, I felt old emotions begin to resurface and consume me. I prayed, "Father, not again. Tell me this is not happening to Ashlyn again. What do I do?" Angry and afraid to go to the hospital, I pulled into a shopping center parking lot and sobbed uncontrollably. The tears wouldn't stop. After several minutes, I pulled myself together as best I could, got on the freeway and began what turned out to be another seven-week journey at Texas Children's Hospital.

Camron was in the third grade and was, unfortunately, being bounced between his grandmother at our home and friends' homes. Robert had already reported for training camp. Although Camron loved spending time with his friends and their families, he was missing the love and attention from his own.

I should note that Robert and I never formally addressed Ashlyn's syndrome with Camron. As he grew older, our normal was his normal. He was very much aware that Ashlyn was sick, that she went to physical therapy and that she went to the doctor's office a lot. He occasionally asked us questions and we would answer, but we generally did not draw unnecessary attention to her illness. All Camron knew was that Ashlyn was his big sister and he loved her very much.

One thing did happen though, that enabled me to witness (for the first time) what our "normal" looked like through Camron's eyes. He was seven years old and playing in a youth soccer league. I didn't normally take Ashlyn with me to his practices or games (due to weather conditions or inadequate handicapped access). This particular game day, I didn't have a sitter for Ashlyn, so she had to go with me. I found a spot on the side of the field and set up my chair with Ashlyn next to me in her handicap stroller. Camron was playing around with a few kids before the game. The next time I looked up, I noticed he and another teammate were involved in a pretty heavy conversation. They were within earshot, and what I overheard made my heart sink. His teammate asked Camron, "Who's that?" Camron, who was totally oblivious to what or whom he was talking about asked him, "Who's who? What are you talking about?" His teammate, a little more specific, asked again, "Who's that girl?" Camron, still clueless, replied, "What girl?" Once again, irritated and even more specifically, his teammate asked Camron, "Who is that girl with your Mom?" Camron glanced at the sideline of the field located Ashlyn and me and nonchalantly replied, "Oh, that's my sister." Camron's answer evidently didn't satisfy his teammate. I was inconspicuously listening, and curious about what would happen next.

The teammate said the unimaginable.

"Oh. She's ugly."

Shocked and saddened to my core, I chose not to say anything right away. I wanted to see how Camron would handle the situation. It was obvious Camron was caught off guard. His defense was, "That's my sister! Nobody cares! (about his opinion of her being ugly)" The next thing I know, the two of them ran off to go play with the other kids before the start of the game.

Anyone who knows me knows I couldn't and wouldn't hold my tongue. I yelled for Camron to come to me. He ran over and I asked him, "What did your friend say to you?" Camron said, "Nothing." I told him I had overheard the conversation with his teammate, and I wanted to know how he felt about what was said. He said, "Mommy, you're gonna tell his mom, and I don't want him to get in trouble. He didn't mean it." I chose to use this moment as a teaching tool, so I took it upon myself to call his teammate over to me. Camron was likely embarrassed, but I knew that was an opportunity for God's grace and truth to be activated in that child's life. Camron's teammate approached me and I said, "Hey honey! How are you? I understand you wanted to know who Camron's sister was? I'd love for you to meet her. This is Ashlyn. Can you shake her hand?" I picked up Ashlyn's hand for him to shake it. He drew back as if he were afraid and said, "No!"

Another knife to the heart.

Camron watched on, his eyes double their size. I reached for his teammate's hand to hold it and told him there was nothing to be afraid of. "This is Camron's sister; my daughter. We love Ashlyn. Do you see your Mom pregnant with your new baby brother or sister? Well, I'm sure you already love the baby and he or she is not even here yet. You have no idea what he or she is going to look like." By this time, his mother was tuned into what was going on, and she listened intently. "That was not a very nice thing to say about Camron's sister or anyone else for that matter. God made us all. Different colors, shapes and sizes and He loves us all. Think about the things you say about people. You wouldn't want anyone calling your brother or sister names, would you? It would hurt your feelings, wouldn't it?" "Yes ma'am," he said. I replied, "Okay, good. Now, you boys go play your game and win!"

His mom walked over, mortified at what she'd just heard. She apologized profusely. I told her apologies weren't necessary, and that Ashlyn and I had used that opportunity to teach her son and Camron that differences in people are not to be feared.

His mom is still one of my best friends to this day. If Camron had been the one saying not-so-nice things about someone, I would have expected her to correct him. I was grateful for Camron's response, and grateful for his teammate's ability to receive the correction I gave him. It really does take a village to raise children.

Since Ashlyn had been transferred to the PICU, Camron was not permitted to see her. Hospital policy required visitors to be at least thirteen years old to visit patients in PICU. Two weeks had passed since Ashlyn had been admitted to the hospital. The next five weeks were physically grueling, emotionally draining and mentally challenging for all of us.

Camron went to school every day. He didn't miss a single class. His Head of School, teachers and other parents were so willing to help with whatever we needed: prayer, shuttling Camron to and from school, allowing him to stay overnight at their homes, tutoring...there was no request too big. They accommodated us with readiness and love. Nothing was off limits when it came to these wonderful people helping my family and me. I was (and remain today) incredibly grateful.

During that seven-week hospital stay, I was away from Camron a lot. It was difficult as a mother to manage how both my children needed me in completely different ways. I was so drained from watching Ashlyn go through her battle, I just wanted to shut down.

Before long, things took a turn for the worse. Robert was traveling between San Antonio and Houston regularly. In a show of kindness and rarely seen professionalism, the team executives and coaches told him he would "lose his job" if he didn't stay in Houston until Ashlyn was stable. We appreciated his employer's attempt at keeping it light. It helped to know they understood the toll all the back-and-forth was taking on Robert and all of us. I was grateful to Coach Popavich and the San Antonio Spurs organization for being so supportive during such a stressful time.

Ashlyn not only had pneumonia, but she had also contracted two staph infections. Surgery was necessary to drain fluid from her right lung. While in surgery, the doctors became concerned about a heart irregularity. After surgery, her blood pressure dropped to a dangerously low level. This was one of her many near-death experiences.

In her crowded room, I stood at the foot of her bed next to Robert, my mother and Lelia. We all watched as she literally changed colors before our eyes. There was so much commotion in that room. Doctors and nurses were constantly coming in and going out. The monitor alarms were sounding, and respiratory staff was transporting equipment. One of the doctors gave a verbal order for us to leave. The nurses had begun to usher us out when one of the nurses softly said, "Mrs. Horry, all we can do is pray for her. She is a very sick little girl." I remember praying and saying to God, "It is my desire to take Ashlyn home from this hospital, but if she's tired of fighting, I know I will have to release her. Father, let Your will be done."

God answered my prayer once again and spared our daughter's life. Ashlyn came home the week of Thanksgiving and recuperated nicely. However, she still required a significant amount of medical attention, care and follow-up doctor visits.

Just when I thought things were settling down a bit, Camron started acting out in school.

Excellent.

So, I had parent/teacher conferences two weeks in a row. His attitude toward school had gone from one extreme to the other. He had been fibbing about homework, not turning work in when it was due, daydreaming in class and not completing his work. All of which was adversely affecting his grades. I tried every approach to get a handle on the situation. I talked casually to Camron, thinking he would open up and tell me what was on his mind. It seemed to be an effective strategy, but he continued doing things he knew were wrong. I had never before been at my wits' end when it came to Camron. He's a really a good kid, so the behavior was out of character for him. I didn't know what else to do. I felt frustrated and helpless. But I was willing to do whatever it took to get Camron back on track. Usually, that situation would include both parents coming to a resolution. I vented my frustrations to Robert, but I was not necessarily looking for him to partner with me with decisions regarding the children. It had become a dysfunctional "normal" for me to manage those scenarios alone. It wasn't something that was verbally communicated. It just developed that way with Robert being away most of the time.

After really thinking about Camron's behavior, I came to the conclusion that the family's focus had solely been on Ashlyn. He was simply asking for attention in his own way. Poor kid. After all the chaos, I can't say I blamed him. Who wouldn't want a little extra attention after managing all that stress at eight years old? With Robert gone so much, he had to grow up faster than most because I needed him to be a "big boy." Through all the troubling circumstances we were always mitigating, without knowing we had done so, we required Camron to be independent. Considering that I had two children at two different ends of the health and needs spectrum, it was often difficult and frustrating to balance time between both of them. Once I realized the source of Camron's acting out, I understood that I had to be just as patient and attentive with him as I was with Ashlyn. As financially advantaged as we were, there were times when Camron couldn't participate in certain things or go certain places because I didn't have help with Ashlyn. Many times, the activities that he wanted to take part in clashed with her schedule. Everybody's life revolved around Ashlyn's. She was on a feeding schedule, a sleep schedule, a bathroom schedule and so on. My heart ached for Camron because, in many ways, it was as if he was an only child. There was only so much interaction he could have with his sister because of her medical situation. Camron has a big heart and has always been a real trouper.

From day one, he was always Ashlyn's "big little brother," and I believe that no matter how challenging the situation got for us, Camron gained life tools that will yield him a great reward. Being Ashlyn's brother armed him with life lessons many children don't have the privilege of getting. I understood that, despite the demands Ashlyn's health put on our family as a whole, he needed attention as well. I realized Camron's acting out was the best way he could get the message across. I was in a constant state of prayer and supplication.

CHAPTER EIGHT

GLAMOROUS GROWING PAINS

*"Purpose transforms mistakes into miracles and
disappointments into testimonies."*
~Dr. Myles Munroe

I don't minimize the importance of being a mother, however I am clear that motherhood is one of many purposes I am to fulfill. Empty Nest Syndrome is not in my future. My challenge had always been in committing to anything outside of family because Ashlyn demanded my time. Nevertheless, despite my unusual circumstances, I always want to stay active, mentally stimulated and productive. When I hit a wall in these areas, I refer to it as my "mini identity crisis."

I've had a lot of them.

My desires ranged from owning a business to completing my degree - and countless other aspirations in between. To some extent, I was still very much (mentally) the wide-eyed, undecided college student I was when I got pregnant with Ashlyn. I also knew that, although I did have my whole life ahead of me, time was most certainly ticking away.

The opportunity to establish a business never materialized, but in August 2008, I put on a cap and gown and walked across the stage in Coleman Coliseum to receive my Bachelor of Arts degree from the University of Alabama. Conquering this milestone created an amazing sense of accomplishment and empowerment. And, for the first time in years, I felt I was in control of something. Had I finished school in 1993 (the original plan), it would not have had the same meaning as it did in 2008. I look back now and question whether I was even ready for college immediately after high school, but I went because that's what was expected of me. Even though my original plan was derailed, I'm glad I had more life experiences and a greater sense of what was important to me by the time I'd finally graduated college.

Once I got my degree, having the support of my family and Robert's family meant significantly more to me. That day will forever be particularly special because my children were there to share it with me - and my father was watching from heaven and smiling. I knew that for sure.

That transition allowed me to look at life through a slightly different lens. Eight years ago, I started taking an annual "girl trip" with a wonderful group of women. We have traveled to some spectacular places that I've only dreamed of visiting. Each time we went though, I had to fight off feelings of guilt. I was plagued with "What if?" thoughts. I had to cancel at the last minute a couple times when Ashlyn was ill. My moments with friends were stolen. A movie or a conversation over tea, or a glass of wine with friends were all meticulously calculated outings. I perceived those social desires as selfishness, not realizing that it was okay to give myself permission to relax a bit. I had developed an internal struggle regarding the need for balance. I often sought confirmation from Robert that it was okay for me to go when I did want a couple hours with friends. I counted on him to give me the permission I couldn't give myself.

Selfishness is not okay with me. I don't tolerate it from others, which means I am especially intolerant of it in myself. But I have learned that a balanced level of self-preservation is necessary for every human to function properly. I am a born nurturer. Most mothers are designed that way. We naturally position ourselves last on the long list of priorities. For mothers, no task is ever completed. There are no days off, and there are no sick days. There are no leaves-of-absence or pay raises. As difficult as we may think motherhood is, once it actually happens in our lives, we end up wishing it were that easy.

That fact is magnified immeasurably as it relates to caring for a special-needs child.

Nevertheless, motherhood is the most rewarding and fulfilling job I can imagine. That being said, burnout has to be intentionally avoided. That means staying prayed up and implementing things that provide balance. I needed a lot of help doing that.

Robert and the kids had become my world, so when those areas were challenged, I felt as though the world was coming to an end. But by God's grace, He sustained me. By choosing to ignore what my feelings were telling me about my circumstances and my dreams, I realized the importance of "the process." I have learned that the lesson isn't in reaching the destination. It's in the journey, which requires embracing the places you don't want to embrace - in shining light on the dark places in the soul. The only way to successfully do that is by keeping the *mind* renewed with the word of God. This is not my opinion. It's not even a fact. It is *truth*. And in saying that, I am not attempting to convince. I am only obeying the call to present.

In the growth process, pressing forward fosters a discovery of who you really are, and what qualities you authentically possess. I've heard the process of self-discovery described many times as a process of pulling away layers. I've frequently felt completely torn down, trying to balance my life and find meaning. After each devastating setback though, God rebuilt me (are you noticing a pattern yet?).

My life's setbacks have given me the revelation that He doesn't leave us where we are if we are open to surrendering to His will. But saying "no" to my own free will and "yes" to God's will is the one thing every human being since Adam and Eve have in common. But God, in His infinite wisdom, doesn't fight with us. He nudges. He urges. He convicts. But He doesn't force. He wants us to willingly surrender the free will He gave us when it is in our best interest to do so. Being able to discern these surrender moments requires deep consecration with God – which happens through a steady diet of His word. Not out of vain repetition or legalistic obligation, but out of an eager desire for more of Him.

I have always had that desire.

That desire got me through my unplanned pregnancy. That desire got me through Ashlyn's birth. That desire got me through the scariest times with respect to Ashlyn's diagnosis. That desire guided me though the lessons to be learned and keeps me running my race. I know there are levels to reach and a destiny to fulfill. As evidenced by my story, fulfilling our destiny requires helping someone else to fulfill their destiny. Emotions - which are, at best undependable and at worst liars - have to be put aside to accomplish the mission. It's not easy, but it is possible.

God's word says, "Being confident of this very thing, that He which hath begun a good work in you, will perform it until the day of Jesus Christ." - Philippians 1:6.

I cling to that Scripture every day.

If I had to go back and do anything differently, I wouldn't. I can be naïve and process things in my own time, but I've made peace with how God created me. I know that when my flesh is weak, the Holy Spirit living in me is strong and He never sleeps. I have been walking in victory even (and especially) when I didn't feel victorious. That is how I understand God's amazing grace.

Ashlyn had been a God given gift to everyone with whom she came in contact. She kept me humble. Love is infectious. When you give it, it comes back and gives back. Ashlyn has given back so much love and joy. I learned from her every day. She embodied the word "happy." Happiness and joy were all she knew. Other than her physical condition, she knew no stress or sadness. She was a living, breathing example of Heaven on earth. I was overcome by the warmth of her presence.

I know I was appointed by God to take care of her. It's my prayer that when I see Him I will hear Him say, "You have done well, my good and faithful servant."

~PERCEPTION VS. REALITY~

One morning, I took Ashlyn to school just as I had every other morning. She was in fifth grade, and attending the neighborhood elementary school that was about four miles from our home. I walked her to her classroom, which was a portable located at the back of the school. As I was leaving,

I passed several classrooms. In the last classroom there were three teachers standing together, talking before the bell rang. As I approached them I cheerfully said, "Good Morning!" They each returned the greeting. I walked past them and heard one of the ladies say (in what she thought was a whisper), "It must be nice to drop off your kid and go to the gym or go shopping." Her judgmental words penetrated to my core. She could've said worse but I was dumbfounded she would say anything at all. To this day, that teacher doesn't know I heard her.

I was crushed.

I couldn't get to my car fast enough. In fact, my walk changed to a jog. I wanted to get to my car before the water that had welled up in my eyes ran down my face. Once I got to my car, I got in, locked the doors and sobbed hysterically in the school parking lot. The hurt feelings quickly shifted to anger. "If she only knew," I thought. I took that anger and that private thought and tucked them away. What I didn't know then was that the anger would rear its head one day.

A few weeks later, I was again walking Ashlyn to her classroom. I had to walk past the same teacher who made the hurtful comment. I resisted the temptation to "get her told," because my spiritual conviction would only allow the question, "What would Jesus do?" (Once again, the claim that Christianity "is for the weak" is annihilated.) I took the high road, as I always try to do. I smiled (painfully) and said "Good morning." She smiled and responded cheerfully in kind. That incident taught me that people can - with ease - behave with unthinkable insensitivity and be completely oblivious to the way they show up for others. I realized that she had a misperception of me (as do many others) based on external factors, and she took an action (speaking something she shouldn't have spoken) based on that misperception. What she didn't know was that her insensitive comment ignited a productive anger in me. That anger launched me in the direction that I needed to go.

Author Julia Cameron explains in her book *The Artist's Way* that anger is fuel. It serves as a guide. In the mind of a rational human being, when anger occurs, it is a sign that boundaries have been crossed. Whether or not that anger becomes a productive tool is a choice we make. The Bible says to "Be angry, and do not sin" (Ephesians 4:26 NKJV). With all that in mind, I knew God had a specific outcome planned for that teacher and me. I knew something good would come from it - I just didn't know how or when that good would manifest. The only thing I knew for certain was that God doesn't make mistakes and whatever the plan, it was for the best and it was to bring Him Glory. As a result of this situation, a fire on the inside of me had been ignited. I had made a decision not to allow that anger to infuriate me, but propel me to turn it into something positive. I was determined to make that fire a light for Ashlyn and me.

~SHOES~

Ashlyn's growth patterns were consistently slow. She was the shortest child among her peers at school. That slow development included her feet. From a baby until she started walking at age seven, I had no problem finding shoes for her. It was like buying shoes for a doll. Her shoes became more of a fashion statement. But once she began walking, finding shoes for her became increasingly difficult. Ashlyn's feet were not only short in length, but they were also exceptionally narrow. Throughout her teen years, her shoes were toddler size. Her feet were so narrow that, even in a narrow shoe, they slid around creating thick calluses on the bottoms of her feet and causing severe trauma to her toes and toenails. It's amazing how we can take something like shoes for granted, but this was a major concern for her physical therapist and me. I typically bought her tennis shoes because she needed that type of foot support. She also wasn't coordinated enough to wear sandals or flip-flops. Safety was always an issue with respect to Ashlyn's mobility.

Although these issues were challenging, I am eternally grateful for how God brought us through them, while keeping Ashlyn as comfortable as possible.

~THE MEDICAL REVELATION: 1P36 DELETION SYNDROME~

In December 2007, Robert and I received a second letter from the Department of Molecular and Human Genetics at Baylor College of Medicine. This letter further confirmed that Ashlyn's Chromosome Microarray Analysis (CMA) revealed she had a missing piece (deletion) on Chromosome #1. What was new about this second letter is that Ashlyn's condition had a new name. That name is 1p36 Deletion Syndrome. But mostly, the letter merely reiterated in writing what Ashlyn (and I) had already been living every day for fifteen years. The letter made me emotional, but served as a major breakthrough - for Ashlyn, our family and I'm sure for many others. Their research also provided vital information for people who care for those living with 1p36 Deletion Syndrome. The information helps caregivers to better understand and cope on a day-to-day basis. This is what we learned about our daughter:

WHAT IS 1P36 DELETION SYNDROME?

1p36 Deletion Syndrome is a genetic condition caused by a missing part of chromosome #1. The word "Syndrome" means a collection of features that consistently occur together. The notation "p36" indicates that the missing piece is on the short arm (p) of chromosome 1 at band 36. 1p36 Deletion Syndrome is estimated to occur in approximately 1 in 5,000 to 1 in 10,000 individuals.

CHARACTERISTICS OF 1P36 DELETION SYNDROME

Facial Characteristics - These include a large, late-closing anterior fontanel ("soft spot") deep set eyes, small palpebral fissures (eyes), low set ears, pointed chin, microcephaly (small head size) and flat nasal bridge. Cleft lip and/or cleft palate have been seen in 17%. However, the presence of these features, as well as other facial findings, is quite variable.

GROWTH AND FEEDING

The majority (85%) of children with 1p36 Deletion have growth delays and problems gaining weight. In children with severe feeding difficulties, alternative medical interventions (such as tube feeding or dietary management) may be required in order to obtain optimum nutrition.

NEUROLOGICAL MANIFESTATIONS

Approximately 55%-60% of children with 1p36 Deletion had a history of seizures; with 50% (15 out of 31) having chronic seizures (epilepsy) requiring continued anti-convulsing medications. In addition to the syndrome, many infants will also have low muscle tone (hypotonia). Low muscle tone may further make it difficult for children to reach their developmental milestones on time. Muscle tone may improve with physical therapy.

COGNITION AND BEHAVIOR

Nearly all children with 1p36 Deletion Syndrome have shown some degree of developmental delay and/or cognitive disability (mental retardation). Speech is often more delayed than other skills (such as rolling, walking, etc.). Since the description of this condition is relatively recent, it is difficult to predict the full spectrum of cognitive abilities in children and adults with 1p36 Deletion. In addition to the cognitive disabilities that children with 1p36 deletion may have, there are reports that as many as 55% will also have some behavior problems.

These problems have been described as self-injurious behavior problems (hitting self, biting self), and general abusive behaviors with banging and hitting.

CARDIAC (HEART) MANIFESTATIONS

Approximately 45% of infants with 1p36 Deletion will have a heart problem. This problem may be structural and/or functional.

VISION OR EYE PROBLEMS

Several different vision or eye problems have been reported in children with 1p36 Deletion. The incidence of vision problems range from 75%-85% in different studies. Vision problems may be corrected with the use of glasses or other interventions.

HEARING PROBLEMS

Hearing impairment has been identified in 55%-80% of children with 1p36 Deletion Syndrome.

OTHER COMPLICATIONS

Hypothyroidism (low thyroid hormone) has been found in approximately 20% of children. Therefore, it is recommended that thyroid function tests be performed at birth, 6 months, and annually thereafter.

HOW IS 1P36 DELETION TREATED?

Currently, there is no specific treatment or cure for this condition. The approach to the management of children with chromosome 1p36 Deletions is similar to all children who have a complicated medical condition.

It was a monumental relief to have tangible clinical research definitively answering questions and validating our reality. However, this validating information did not rid me of the isolation I was experiencing. Nor did it provide solutions to the challenges Ashlyn and I had to manage. For instance, I needed a pamphlet of information to instruct me on her food and eating challenges, puberty and where to buy her shoes.

Over the years, I'd tried many strategies to get Ashlyn to eat. I tried encouraging her to explore different tastes. I tried sitting her at the dinner table to send the message that it was time to eat. I tried showing her different fruits - by taking bites myself - to demonstrate that good food goes in the mouth. I showed her the motion of chewing. To show her swallowing, I put her hand on my throat, in the hope she would relate to the mechanic. Nothing worked.

It was difficult to accept the fact that Ashlyn wouldn't eat. Her therapist and I tried for years to create improvement with her feeding. There were some moments of improvement, but then a respiratory infection would set her back. It was a frustrating cycle. Finally, her speech therapist said she felt Ashlyn had reached a plateau regarding eating by mouth. The speech therapist agreed to continue treating Ashlyn, but only to work on oral motor for muscle strength, verbal sounds and speaking syllables. Her suggestion was that we agree to terminate the incorporation of food in her sessions. That was a big blow, but I understood. It wasn't that Ashlyn was being completely defiant and not wanting to learn (although I'm fairly certain there was a bit of that happening, too). Her defiance came from the fact that she anatomically could not tolerate food. Since her epiglottis was completely removed, there was no sure way of protecting her airway (not even from her own saliva).

When I spoke to Ashlyn's Ear Nose and Throat Otolaryngologist, she said there are many cases of chronic smokers who have developed cancer, which in many cases led to the removal of the epiglottis. The difference between these people and Ashlyn is they eventually adjust to the absence of the epiglottis and are still able to eat. They have a frame of reference (similar to muscle memory) and, based on that frame of reference, they learn to protect the airway without an epiglottis. Ashlyn however, was never able to establish that frame of reference.

The simple function of eating is another thing (like buying shoes) we all take for granted. I never thought of eating as a learned behavior. Many of us find comfort - and even develop relationships - in association with food. I am no exception. In fact, I would "stand in the gap" for Ashlyn's not being able to eat!

I joke about it, but the stresses of caring for Ashlyn created an open door for my own body image issues. My weight fluctuated for many years, and I continue to work on establishing peace in that area. People deal with stress differently. Some people overeat or become emotional eaters. Some people shut down and don't eat at all. In my case, my eating habits depend on the degree of the stress I experience. My being the primary caregiver for our daughter created a consistent level of anxiety. The high stress level became my "normal." I adapted to it. In an attempt to ignore and cushion the pain of loneliness, frustration and depression, I sometimes comforted myself with food. From a physical perspective, I fully understand how important it is to be healthy for those depending on me, and I am by no means a glutton, nor am I morbidly obese. I simply spent many years not being at optimal health. I realize that I cannot go all day without eating (because I'm busy), and I cannot eat the wrong foods late at night. I know those habits will have an adverse affect on my metabolism. That was the cause of my weight gain and, subsequently, my disappointment when the weight doesn't miraculously fall off when I begin healthy habits. I make a conscious effort every day to do what I know is right so I am able to give my children my best. Making healthy choices is every parent's responsibility, and I'm grateful for the conviction that comes when I fall short in that area.

I was always conscious of feeding Ashlyn in public. Because she fed through a tube, I was cognizant of the fact that not everyone was familiar with seeing someone eat that way. Frankly, seeing someone feed that way can be a bit much - especially when seeing it for the first time. In fact, it was a bit much for me the first time I saw it. I would usually either feed her in my car or, if that wasn't feasible, I'd make sure she was covered with a blanket when I fed her in public. What was funny to me was when

I was on an airplane and had to feed her. I got all kinds of looks, and people had no problem staring. I handled others' insulting behavior by smiling and staying focused on getting my daughter fed. After all, I suppose it did look strange to see an oversized syringe attached to a long tube, funneling PediaSure into a child's stomach.

So much for the *glamorous* lifestyle most people associate with being the wife of a professional athlete.

Glamour was not my reality. And, with the airport security changes after September 11, 2001, traveling became a much more stressful ordeal. The extra time it took to get through security checkpoints was just the beginning. For Ashlyn, Camron and me, travel included carrying two changes of clothes in case Ashlyn had any accidents, her Pull-Ups®, her food (PediaSure and Ensure), water, her meds and her nebulizer machine for breathing treatments. Everything was packed in her carry-on bag. I was always flustered and damp with perspiration from undressing, removing shoes, unpacking the laptop and making sure Camron was prepared to go through security. Meanwhile, Ashlyn would be whisked away in her handicapped stroller by a TSA employee (also known as a stranger). She would then be taken to the holding area until I walked through security and gathered my belongings. I was managing the organized chaos while trying to keep an eye on both children - who were in two separate places - and complying with the TSA agent impatiently demanding to rifle through my bag. After several minutes being separated from Ashlyn and Camron, I'd tell the TSA agent I needed to be with my children, and that the bag will have to wait a minute. I would then gather Camron and our belongings, and walk several security stations over to where Ashlyn was sitting with said stranger. Now, not seeing a familiar face at a busy airport security checkpoint would be traumatizing to a child without disabilities. I can't imagine what that was like for Ashlyn. I'd often yell to her from across the room, "Mommy's here, Ashlyn. I'll be right there." I'd get the stares, but her comfort would always usurp any embarrassment I felt.

When I would finally make it to her with Camron in tow, the TSA agent would say, "Ma'am, I'm just going to pat her down and wipe down her chair. Is she sensitive in any place I should know about before I begin the procedure?" By that time, Ashlyn was usually extremely agitated. She would buck her stroller and hit the person trying to touch on her. I'd stand there watching the fiasco thinking there had to be a better way. As harrowing as what I just described sounds, add to it the fact that there were different procedures in every airport. That escalated the frustration level immeasurably. I couldn't ever establish a regular routine with travel. I was always on-guard; expecting the unexpected. Additionally, many times the security agents weren't specialists in patience and compassion. They considered it an inconvenience to have to deal with a special-needs child. Managing Ashlyn, Camron and the attitudes of airport personnel was a always stress-management challenge.

Our frequent travel to Los Angeles (to see Robert) always began first with prayer, asking God to pilot the pilot and get us (and everyone) safely to our destinations. Cam had his DVD player (and you think a flotation device is a lifesaver), and Ashlyn had her pillow. She'd fall asleep every time on planes.

One time after the plane had taken off, I looked up from my magazine and noticed Ashlyn was sweating like crazy, going in and out of consciousness and her lips were turning pale. I couldn't panic, and had to think quickly. I checked to see if she was breathing. She was, but her breathing was alarmingly shallow. I began taking off her clothes, leaving just her sports bra and Pull-Ups® on. I positioned the air vent directly on her while shouting her name to check her level of awareness. I'm not certain, but I think the person seated behind me pushed the flight attendant button. The next thing I knew, the flight attendant was ushering two gentlemen toward my seat to offer assistance. They were both firemen. Thank God! I didn't want to scare Camron (or anyone else), but inside I was freaking out. I tried to stay in control. "Ashlyn, wake up! Wake up! Look at Mommy," I kept repeating. We had never experienced anything like that before. The fact that it happened on a plane exacerbated the panic. One of the firemen asked about her medical history as he was checking for a pulse and lifting her eyelid to see the positioning of her eyes. The other fireman went to get an oxygen tank and mask. Once the oxygen mask was positioned, someone yelled out, "Get her some orange juice." The fireman didn't object, so the flight attendant got the juice. I gave it to her through her G-tube and within minutes she was looking around at everyone standing over her. As she began laughing, I took a deep breath, exhaled and continued to sweat. I was in utter disbelief. One of the firemen exchanged seats with the person across the aisle from me to be close by in case Ashlyn had another episode before we landed. I was most grateful. Once I realized Ashlyn was herself again, I put on her a change of clothes (now you see why I needed so many supplies in her carry-on bag). The clothes she'd had on earlier were drenched with sweat. Thankfully, the remainder of the flight was peaceful. Camron continued watching his DVD as if nothing had ever happened. Children are resilient.

Since that first episode, Ashlyn had a few more exactly like the first one - and each time she had them on planes. I still am not certain of the cause. My guess is that either the change in the cabin pressure or the changes in the cabin temperature may have triggered the episodes. Regardless of the cause, the experiences were not fun but they were manageable. When it happened, I would do what we did the first time: take off her top and give her orange juice immediately. Her color would return to normal and she would go on smiling and trying to take the Sky Mall catalog out of the seat pocket in front of her.

Speaking of embarrassing moments, I'll share a doozie of a shopping trip to Target - one of which I only have myself to blame for my embarrassment. It was a Sunday morning. We had gone to church and I decided to stop and get a gift card for Camron to take to a birthday party. Target was on the way home. It seemed like a good idea because, once I got home, I often didn't want to go back out. Camron asked if we should go home first so Ashlyn could potty. I should have listened to him.

Out of the mouths of babes…

We got in the store, and Ashlyn was pushing the cart. A woman passed us and complimented Ashlyn's dress.

Just as she gushed over the dress, Ashlyn simultaneously peed through her Pull-Ups® onto the floor. All I heard was water splashing, and it didn't take me long to realize what was happening. I sent Camron to find the paper towels aisle. My head was barraged with thoughts. We couldn't just walk away. Someone was sure to slip and fall, and I couldn't bear the thought of causing an unnecessary accident. So, Ashlyn and I just stood there waiting for Camron to return with paper towels. It seemed like five hours had passed. While waiting for him, Ash and I saw a woman we knew from her school. Of course, after the usual pleasantries, I explained why Ashlyn and I were standing in the middle of the aisle. God sends angels when you need them. The woman interrupted her shopping to help me. She went to the bathroom and brought paper towels back. Meanwhile, Camron still had not returned. As soon as we'd cleaned up, he came down the aisle shouting, "Mom, I couldn't find the paper towels!" My guess was that he was probably in the toy department playing a video game he was planning to ask me to buy.

Needless to say, we left the store as quickly as possible.

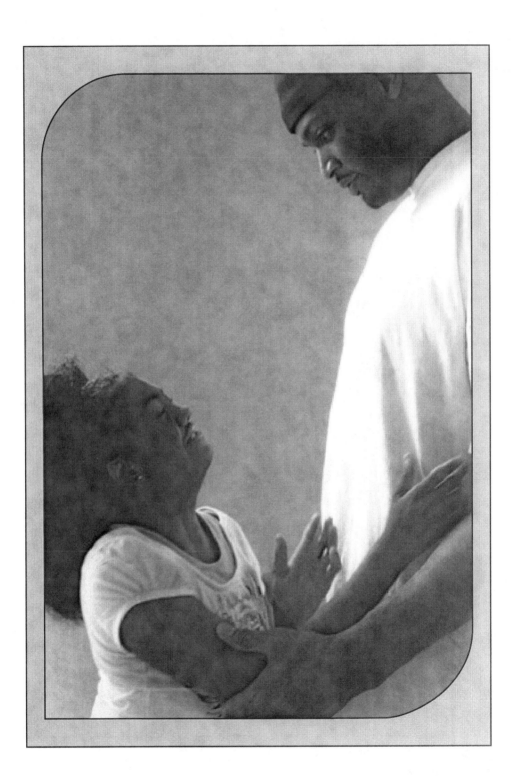

CHAPTER NINE

Glamorous "Sweet Sixteen"

*"Success can make you go one of two ways. It can
make you a prima donna — or it can smoothe the
edges, take away the insecurities,
let the nice things come out."*
~Barbara Walters

Ashlyn was beaming with joy in her lavender dress and satin sash. Her long, thick, curly hair was pulled up in one ponytail with ringlets hanging from the crown of her head. It was a special occasion, which called for the best of the best. I felt as I would imagine the mother of a bride would feel as I put her diamond earrings in her ears. They matched the sparkle in her eyes. She knew that day was hers. She owned it. The excitement had been building. I flew in an amazing photographer to capture every detail of the day. After all, a girl's "Sweet Sixteen" only happens once.

We walked down the stair and Ashlyn made her grand debut at her "Sweet Sixteen" birthday party. There was a fairly high percent chance of rain predicted for the day, so I rented a tent hoping the festivities would not be ruined. That outdoor party was going to happen; come rain, hail, sleet or snow. Gratefully, it didn't rain.

I'd hired a D.J. and spent hours creating the perfect playlist for her perfect day. The party included a catered buffet. And of course, the color scheme was Ashlyn's favorite color - purple. Ashlyn was surrounded by the love of family, close friends, physicians, therapists, teachers and paraprofessionals. I wanted everyone who had played a role in Ashlyn's life there. It was more than a birthday celebration. It was also a sincere show of gratitude to everyone - my "village" - who had helped me care for Ashlyn.

Ashlyn was bursting with joy and excitement. She let us know with her body language that she knew every person there. She hugged countless people, danced for a few minutes and blew out her candles after we all sang "Happy Birthday" to her. She hugged more people and even lovingly hit a few (sometimes Ashlyn's hitting was an expression of endearment). It was an exhausting day and she was beyond tired.

Because Ashlyn had a mind of her own (and a stubborn one, at that), she let go of my hand during the party and walked toward the house to go inside. I realized what she was doing and ran to catch up with her. I figured she must have needed a diaper change. We walked inside, and Ashlyn aggressively headed for the staircase. She could not go up without assistance, but she was clearly determined to do exactly that. I was desperately trying to figure out if she was in pain, hungry or wet. We got to her room and I guided her toward her bathroom. She quickly pulled away from me and went the opposite direction toward her bed. With guests still at our home, Ashlyn had decided she'd had enough and climbed into her bed, dress and all, for a nap. It was one of the most hilarious things she'd ever done. I didn't waste any brain cells trying to figure that one out. The girl was sixteen and clearly telling us, "It's my party, and I'll nap if I want to!" I told the remaining guests that the birthday girl had had enough.

It had turned out to be a beautiful day. We had about fifty guests, and it was a day to remember. I was a proud mom that day. I marvel when I reflect on how she had defeated the odds once again – simply by turning sixteen. I reflected on how the doctors grimly advised me of her life expectancy. No one - except God - knew she'd one day be the belle of her ball.

I believe all things happen at the appropriate time. With advances in modern medicine, our country's health care issues and the eroding stigma around disabilities, this is the perfect season for Ashlyn's story to be told. When the doctors gave me the news that my child's life would be different than I had imagined and planned, I would never have believed it was possible to reach a place of peace and contentment. Against all odds, Ashlyn attended school every day that her respiratory system would allow. She had walked with and without assistance.

She uttered her version of the words *bye-bye, purple, book, brother, potty, papa,* and *mama*. She understood enough to shake her head "no." She used some sign language to communicate. She responded to simple commands. And all of that progress left me in awe at what God had done through love, nurturing and the strategic placement of gifted professionals who helped get Ashlyn reach that miraculous milestone.

I pray for the blessing of consistent progress in other children with special needs like Ashlyn.

~The Ashlyn Horry Foundation~

While the Horry name has been synonymous with "big shots" and championships in the sports world, in the game of life, Ashlyn Horry is the true champion of the Horry family. I have a passion for children like Ashlyn to have the quality of life they deserve. I see the need to provide information and support to families in similar situations. Because of that need, I founded *The Ashlyn Horry Foundation* (AHF). We envision children with medically diagnosed disabilities will have the same quality of life as children without disabilities. Our vision is to enhance existing resources for disabled youth by providing opportunities for economic relief and medical research. AHF is committed to providing community initiatives focusing on children's disabilities and caregivers while providing resources for development and empowerment regardless of economic status, race, religion or creed.

The specific objective of AHF is to serve as a resource for disabled youth while supporting initiatives pertaining to their quality of life, education and social well-being. Its purpose is also to heavily impact local community projects and impact national level projects in the future. I established Ashlyn's foundation hoping it would give me an outlet for channeling my passion and experiences raising a special-needs child. I want to help others in identical or similar situations. AHF is the result of my redirecting – in a positive way - the negative experience I had with the teacher at Ashlyn's school. I thank God for that teacher's erroneous perception of my life. The life I have lived has been incredibly challenging, but also deeply rewarding. I'm very proud to be able to leave a legacy in my daughter's honor.

To me, that's glamorous.

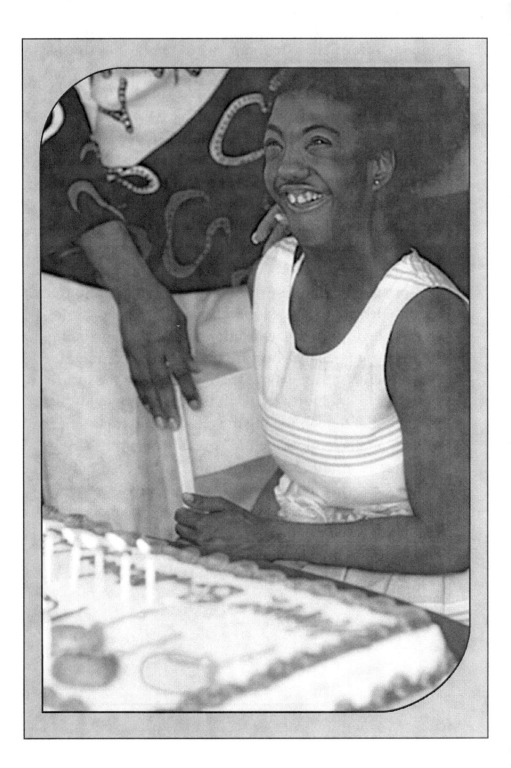

CHAPTER TEN

GLAMOROUS LIFE

"The pen that writes your life story
must be held in your own hand."
~Irene C. Kassorla

The day-to-day grind got tiring, but the perseverance and determination of a young girl, small in stature and large in spirit, inspired me. As I entered another phase of life preparing for a new decade with a teenager and a "tweenager," I found myself thinking more about my age. I also thought about the kids getting older - particularly Ashlyn. I had already been making decisions that would affect the next couple years. One of which was obtaining legal guardianship for Ashlyn as an eighteen-year-old. That thought had never occurred to me. Growing up, all I had ever seen was people graduate from high school, turn eighteen, go to college, get a job, get married and start a family (preferably, in that order).

Those "rules" of young adulthood didn't apply to Ashlyn. I wondered what she would do after graduating from high school. Would she go to an assisted living community? Would she go to an adult daycare? What would become of her private therapy? What about physician transitions from pediatrics to a primary care physician? There was so much to consider. Under "normal" circumstances, I would be helping her plan her future in college and, eventually, helping her plan her wedding. I was still planning her future, but in a different way. I was planning a bright future, tailored just for her.

One day, I was dropping the kids off at school when Camron asked, "Mom, if something were to happen to you, who's gonna take care of Ashlyn?" That question left me buried in a whirlwind of thought and emotion. I reluctantly answered him saying, "Sweetie, Ashlyn will be in good hands if anything were to ever happen to Mommy. Don't you worry about that." I was concerned about my young son having such a deep thought. I didn't want to think about it. At all.

Changes were not only occurring right before my eyes in my children, but also in society. While raising Ashlyn and Camron, I became acutely aware of our society's obsession with consumption; consumed with taking and getting. It saddens me. I believe life is so much more than what we physically see, and so much richer than bank accounts can hold. The beauty in life is in living with purpose. The lessons we learn and the wisdom we gain are the gifts that keep on giving. I often tell people that Ashlyn taught me more than I could ever teach her. Was I living the life I had dreamed of living? No. But I'm glad I wasn't in control, and that God designed His plan for me exactly as He did.

We all live to find purpose. Houses, cars, clothes, designer bags, jewelry and a closet full of shoes are nice to possess, but life becomes much more fulfilling when driven by purpose rather than things. Acquiring things, by the way, is not a purpose. One's purpose is always rooted in God's preordained tapping. Everyone is tapped with different gifts. Those gifts are the catalysts for fulfilling purpose. The possessions we acquire in the meantime are irrelevant. The evidence of this is the fact that, since the beginning of time, history is riddled with wealthy, famous people who have bought all they can buy and taken their own lives. There isn't a possession on earth that can fill a God-shaped hole.

To that end, people often complimented my cars, clothing and jewelry. While I was grateful for a husband who was a wonderful provider, the truth remained that all my "things" did not erase the pain and agony I experienced raising a special-needs child. Nor did they replenish all the time I spent away from my husband. I made no apologies for how God blessed my family, but the thing about God is that He is no respecter of persons. We all have to endure our fair share of pain and suffering. When real life and fantasy are blurred, negative perceptions can develop. That leads to unfair judgments. No one can control how they're perceived by others, but it's true that perception is reality.

Not necessarily *the* reality, but someone's reality.

I'd worked day and night as have many other stay-at-home moms. However, no one sees the real baggage inside my Louis Vuitton luggage. No one knows how many miles I put on that Mercedes Benz going to and from Texas Children's Hospital and physical therapy. No one knows the rocky roads my Christian Louboutin shoes have tread. But in the eloquent words of Maya Angelou, "…And still I rise."

Because of the knowledge, wisdom, humility and patience that I gained just from having Ashlyn, I wouldn't trade my life for the world. The word *Glamorous* in the title of this book has nothing to do with material possessions. But, some will think it does because that's all their life experiences will allow them to see.

The word *Glamorous* in the title of this book has everything to do with my purpose.

I'd dedicated my life to taking care of a child who couldn't take care of herself. The fact that we lived within a certain tax bracket certainly helped from a financial perspective (I can't imagine attending to Ashlyn's medical needs without the financial provision we've had), but it didn't change the fact that we had a sick child. Glamour, fame, and wealth come with a certain amount of weight and responsibility. "...To whom much is given, of him much is required..." (Luke 12:48 AMP)

~THE ELEPHANT IN THE ROOM~

When writing a memoir, it's possible to become so engrossed in getting it on paper that the reader's perspective is lost. In my case, there are some components of my life that are so painful I wish I could bury them forever. During the writing of this book, my literary agent said she detected something missing. In my mind, she was wrong. I had shared all I felt I needed to share in order to help others who shared a similar situation. But in my heart, I knew I had not. Her advice was to let go and just write it out. She was right. With tears welling in my eyes before we hung up the phone, I knew there was something I had to release for my well being. There was an ever-present hurt that needed to heal. Here goes.

During the first six months Ashlyn was in the hospital, I remember one of the night-shift respiratory therapists making a comment that I have tried to delete from my mind for years. I figured if I put it to rest in my mind and never spoke about it, no life would be given to it.

In casual conversation, the nurse told Robert and me that ninety percent of married couples with special-needs children end up divorced.

I didn't respond, and everything she said after that was white noise. I rejected what she'd said. It didn't matter to me where the statistic came from or whether or not it was true. I purposely blocked her statement out of my head. I was determined not to allow that statistic to be a reality in my marriage.

It's not easy being married to a professional athlete. Couple that with raising a special-needs child and living apart for the sake of that child's medical needs, and you have a perfect storm of division brewing. Back in 2006 while I was grieving the loss of my father, I also began to grieve the very evident downward spiral of my marriage.

I fought hard for my marriage and my family. I prayed and tried everything I could think of to save my marriage. But, I came to the end of my tolerance. There was too much at stake with our children. I didn't want to worsen an already difficult situation with marital strife. Children are intuitive. They know when things aren't right. For everyone's sake, I needed to stop the proverbial bleeding.

I couldn't believe the man I had been with since I was nineteen years old - my college sweetheart and the man I loved and adored deeply - was going to be my former husband. This was one of the hardest decisions I'd ever made in my life. Holding on to hope and fighting for my family till the very end, I quietly left my marriage of nearly twelve years in May 2009.

Because I was a child of divorce, I made a conscious decision (at fifteen years old) that divorce would never be in my future. There was no room for it in my life. The word divorce was not in my vocabulary. It was not an option. Period.

Although my view on the subject was firm, it still happened and our daughter's special needs were not the reason why. My marriage failed because our marital vows, made before God, our family members and friends, were violated to the point of no return. Boy, was I naïve in thinking that marriage in a "traditional" sense of the word would be easily maintained in the environment and lifestyle in which we lived. For me, there were many lessons learned. One big lesson learned was that marriage means different things to different people.

While wrestling with the hurt, anger, humiliation, resentment, failure and the "Why me? Why us?" questions, I had to somehow gain clarity and stay focused on what was most important. Unfortunately, my mental health was not first on the list. My children were first. There was no time to grieve the death of our marriage, or the loss of a dream, which made the pain unbearable. I had two children to raise - one who was dependent on me for the rest of her life. I moved forward with one prayer where my failed marriage was concerned: that God would honor the love, honesty and integrity of my heart during Robert's and my years together, and that our children would know beyond a shadow of a doubt that they were conceived in love and that our love for them deepens as each second passes.

After doing a lot of work on myself and surrendering to my responsibilities as a single mother, I realized I could only take one step at a time.

Despite all the pain, God has been my constant comfort. He has truly blessed me and, after the divorce, I could once again see His faithfulness in my life. My primary focus was my children. Considering everything, there's not one thing I would do differently (except have my marriage work). My literary agent was right. Not including this information in my memoir would have left a gaping hole in my story. Holding on to pain disallows growth. I've released it.

It is my desire that God's face will shine upon those who don't know Him. It is my desire that God will make His presence known whether it be through the words on these pages, or through the life I have lived. Where there are misguided perceptions about the fairytale lifestyle many think accompanies being the wife of a high-profile professional athlete, it is my hope that my story sheds light on a different reality. We all have issues, and they are all relative. But the common denominator is sacrifice. We all pay a price, for who and where we are in life.

CHAPTER ELEVEN

GLAMOROUS FIGHT

*"There are only two ways to live your life. One is
as though nothing is a miracle. The other is
as though everything is a miracle."*
~ Albert Einstein

My checklist for bed every night included pajamas, bed, pillow, blanket and Ashlyn's monitor so I could see and hear her during the night. On Saturday, September 11, 2010, I was startled out of my sleep at 4:55 A.M. to Ashlyn's loud wheezing. Disoriented, I ran to her room finding her in bed with her head tilted back as if she was looking at the ceiling with her shoulders shrugged up to her ears. I thought she was having muscle spasms, so I tried to massage her shoulders. She then whacked me right in the nose. Seriously…she rang my bell. I didn't realize she couldn't breathe and was trying to get oxygen (what a horrible feeling, as a mother, to misread the signs). But there was no time to focus on what I couldn't figure out. I was praying for quick thinking and relied on my maternal instincts.

I managed to get her out of bed and to her special chair so she could sit upright as I gave her a breathing treatment. Two-to-three minutes into the breathing treatment, her eyes were rolling in the back of her head and she started falling forward. If I had not been sitting in front of her, she would have fallen on the floor face first. I threw the breathing treatment mask off of her face, grabbed her pre-packed bag of clothes and raced to the car to get her to the ER. When I went to get Ash out of her chair, she went limp on the floor. It was like holding dead weight. I realized at that point we weren't going to make it to the car, let alone to the ER. I called 911, which I had not done in years. I was trying not to panic. Robert was out of the country working. Neither of our parents was in town. I was trying not to wake Camron up (he was eleven years old at the time). Fortunately, I had a cousin visiting for the weekend. She and her family were contemplating a move to Houston and had appointments with a Realtor to go house hunting. Worst-case scenario, I could leave Camron with her until my neighbor was able to watch him while she and her husband house hunted. I was dizzy with what seemed like a million thoughts happening at one time. But believe it or not, as chaotic as those moments were, there was an underlying peace I cannot begin to explain.

"9-1-1. What's your emergency?" I replied, "I need an ambulance right away. My daughter is having a very difficult time breathing and she's very lethargic. She is dead weight at the moment. I can't lift her. She's fading on me and I'm trying to keep her awake." The voice on the other end asked for my name, my address and Ashlyn's name and age. I answered all her questions. The next voice I heard was Cam's. "Mommy, what's wrong?" I replied, "Ash is not feeling very well, sweetie. Go back to bed. Everything is fine." I was speaking things that weren't as though they were. I was faith-believing. Of course, that wasn't good enough for him. He came further down the stairs and saw his sister lying on the floor breathing shallow breaths. Realizing that I was still holding the phone, and that the 9-1-1 dispatcher was still on the other line, I simply said, "Please hurry!" She still wanted to keep me on the phone. I was getting angry and trying to keep my cool at the same time. I'm not certain I pulled it off.

The doorbell rang. I yelled for Camron to answer it. Under normal circumstances, I would have never let him answer the door - even if I knew who was coming to our home. But, these weren't normal circumstances. The EMT team walked through pushing a gurney to the family room where I was on the floor with Ashlyn. They asked questions about her medical history. I quickly rattled off everything there was to tell over the last sixteen years. I'm not sure if it was nervous energy or because it was second nature, but the EMT's were very clear on Ashlyn's status after my information download.

The action began. They immediately started an I.V. on Ashlyn and gave her oxygen. I sat and watched in disbelief. I was, once again, bereft of natural strength, so I shifted to coping with the situation from a spiritual perspective. Prayers went up as tears fell down. Then, one of the EMT's said, "Ma'am, we are going to have to Life Flight her to the ER. There's not much we can do here. Where would you like for her to go?" Disbelief quickly turned to utter shock. I answered, "I want her to go to Texas Children's Hospital. They know her there."

The scene was surreal as I watched the team carefully lift Ashlyn onto the gurney. They buckled her on and wheeled her out of front door. The dark street lit up with the flashing lights from the ambulance. As they put Ashlyn in the back of the vehicle, I was told to get to the hospital so I could have all the paperwork completed by the time they arrived with her. The helicopter had landed about a mile from my neighborhood in the parking lot of an elementary school.

My next move proved Ashlyn got her stubborn streak from me.

Rather than go straight to the hospital (as instructed), I followed the ambulance to where the helicopter had landed. I tried to drive up to the helicopter. There were two police cars in the middle of the street to deter onlookers (it was 5:30 A.M.). According to the officers, even the patient's mother was considered one to deter. I pleaded with the officer from across the street to let me be with my daughter. I am not a control freak, but knowing my daughter was in such distress created an urgency to be with her. The answer was still a definitive "no." I was told Ashlyn was being "prepped" for the helicopter ride. I asked the officer what that meant. He replied, "Ma'am, if you will just go ahead to the hospital and get all of the paper work done, that will expedite time."

My heart sank. The feeling of helplessness and anger brought on crocodile tears. I pushed the button to let my window up and started the ride to the hospital. I wondered if Ashlyn was awake enough to know that I wasn't there with her. I wondered if she was fighting the team of people trying to help her. All of those thoughts overshadowed the fact that I was driving. I was not mentally present. After driving for about thirty minutes, I had arrived at the hospital. I checked in and was escorted to the room where Ashlyn was with several nurses and respiratory therapists.

Ashlyn was admitted to Texas Children's Hospital - again. Although I had been living in Houston away from family for so long, I was fortunate to have the love, help and support of my close friends (my extended family).

They were by my side in the PICU waiting room. After calling several times, I finally got word to Robert, in China, that Ashlyn had been air lifted to the hospital. The words he spoke to me were short, sweet and they managed to penetrate the most vulnerable part of me. He said, "I'm so sorry I'm not there with you right now. I'm sorry you are going through this. I am coming on the next flight back." I wanted to curl up in the fetal position and cry until I couldn't cry anymore. But there was no time for that. My baby girl needed me.

Robert did get back to Houston. A few days went by and Ashlyn was not out of the woods yet. I basically stayed at the hospital with her, sleeping between her room, the lobby and The Ronald McDonald House, while Robert took care of Camron and saw to it that he was fed, at school every day and doing his homework. He was "Mr. Mom." We needed additional family support, so we flew our parents in. On Monday, September 13, 2010, I decided to check my emails while Ashlyn was calm and sedated. I opened one that read:

> *Keva,*
> *My name is Jay B. and I was the paramedic*
> *on scene Saturday a.m. I was just contacting*
> *you to check up on Ashlyn. In my other job I*
> *am a Christian minister and am praying for*
> *Ashlyn. Please don't hesitate to let me know if*
> *I can be of further assistance to you.*
> *In HIM,*
> *Jay B.*

I was blown away. In addition to being deeply moved by the email, I was also baffled at how he had gotten my email address. That email seemed Divinely delivered. It came at a time I needed it the most. I replied:

> *Oh my gosh, Jay!!! Which one were you? Thank you so much for writing me. I can't tell you how much I appreciate you and your prayers. Saturday was really tough, but God says in His word that the victory is mine! It took SEVERAL hours to get her stabilized (around 4 P.M.). Pneumonia and staph seem to be the culprits. They have her on a host of antibiotics, blood pressure meds and she is on an oscillator. Still heavily sedated and intubated. And she has two central lines in place. They have been trying to wean her off the blood pressure meds but she's not responding well. She is resting well and that is just fine with me. Her body needs it! Things are slow, but there is progress nevertheless. He is Jehovah Rapha our Healer and it is all in His hands. I can't thank you enough!!! God bless you and every life that you touch in Jesus' holy name.*
>
> *Keva Horry*
>
> *P.s.~ I'm in shock that you found me! God totally amazes me!!!!*

It turned out Jay was on the web in search of more information about 1p36 Deletion Syndrome. Through him,

I learned about all the members of the West I-10 EMT in Katy, Texas who took care of Ashlyn the morning of the Life Flight to the hospital. Lora Carter was the Life Flight nurse who "prepped" Ashlyn for the helicopter ride that morning. Ray Sidwell was the team supervisor, and he cared for Ash as well. Not only do I have respect for what they do professionally, but I also have a spiritual bond with them because of Ashlyn.

The days got longer as time passed and they seemed to run together. This was not Ashlyn's first dance with pneumonia and, to make matters worse, she had acquired a staph infection, too. Her left lung had collapsed a number of times. Her team of doctors decided that Robert and I should meet with them to talk about what happened next. We were told Ashlyn had Bronchial Malacia - weakening of the bronchial cartilage. She had an airway protection issue, her left lung was not functioning and she had a restrictive chest wall which affected the title volume (how much air her lungs brought in and out).

The doctors were giving us one of two options for Ashlyn: either trache her and keep her on a ventilator at home, or extubate her and keep her on C-pap until she transitioned without pain into Glory with the Father.

Either way, Robert and I were in agreement that we were not going to play God. It was suggested we keep her in a hospice facility for her final days. Amidst the overwhelm, I kept seeking God's face.

~JOURNAL ENTRY: SUNDAY, OCTOBER 3, 2010~

*Although I went to sleep with my eyes full of
tears, I wake this morning with a heart full
of TRUST! I've read a little in His word and
He (God) tells me to fear not and to be of good
courage. "Yea though I walk through the valley
of death, I will fear no evil, for He is with me.
His rod and His staff comfort and protect me.
He prepares a table before me in the presence
of mine enemies..." "My cup runs over. Surely
goodness and mercy shall follow me all the
days of my life and I (Keva) will dwell in the
house of the Lord forever" ~Psalm 23.
"Be confident in this very thing (Keva) that
He (God) who began a good work will continue
it till the end." Prayer changes everything!
~KDH*

I found the Houston hospice facility that had been
referred to us. Robert met me there. He brought his dad
and we all toured the facility. We were shown a mock room,
which we were told was identical to the room Ashlyn's
would be in. The room was clean, but very cold. The bed
was made up with a single silk rose lying on the pillow.
All I could think was, "She's just a sixteen year old girl!
Why the silk rose?" The rose bothered me. It looked like an
ending. I couldn't believe we were doing this. I was trying
to be strong and I think I held my own fairly well. It was
just an awkward experience. I went to my car and prayed:

*God, I need to feel Your presence right now. I
need you to wrap me in your arms and keep me*

*in that secret place. Prepare me, prepare Robert
and most of all prepare Camron for what will
happen. Whether Ashlyn comes home with us
to Katy, Texas or You call her home to be with
You, prepare us for what is to come.*

Amen.

That same evening, Robert and I decided to have a
family meeting to share with Camron what was going
on with Ashlyn. We felt he needed to know there was a
possibility she wouldn't come home from the hospital.
Ever. I couldn't speak. Robert took over and talked to him
eloquently. If I had been able to speak, I don't believe I
could have done it as effectively as he did. It was a beautiful
for all three of us. Camron sadly asked a few questions,
and then asked to be excused from the room. My heart
ached. But I was not ready to give up hope.

Robert and I later spoke to a personal friend, who
happened to be a spine surgeon, about Ashlyn's prognosis.
We allowed ourselves to get excited after having spoken
to him, thinking some sort of reconstructive surgery
on her rib cage may be the solution to the problems
she was experiencing. Our friend brought in two other
surgeons to solicit their expert opinions on his idea.
"From a surgical standpoint, I don't see anything that
could be done to benefit Ashlyn," one told us. The other
surgeon echoed his opinion. The possibility we wanted to
explore was futile. Every surgeon we brought in (outside
Ashlyn's original team of physicians) was in agreement
that a surgical procedure would not resolve her problem.
The weight on my heart - and the reality of not knowing

what else to do – left me feeling palpably helpless. I don't wish that feeling on any parent.

~JOURNAL ENTRY: FRIDAY, OCTOBER 8, 2010~

Today is the day Ashlyn is scheduled to move from PICU to PCU and taken off the ventilator. Although I'm extremely sad and emotional, I know that God makes NO MISTAKES! I love Ashlyn Ishan Horry and I always will! She has been my angel and I am most grateful for the time that she has been in my life, in Camron's life and in Rob's life. Camron chose to go to school today, but he wrote Ashlyn the SWEETEST letter for me to read to her. It brought me to tears.

Dear Ashlyn,
I really hope that you pass your test because you are the masterpiece in everyone's heart. I'm not going to be there cause I'm at school but everyone else will be there.
Love your brother,
Camron

It's very important to get Ashlyn off of the ventilator so she won't get any more infections. The doctors keep changing the time she'll go off the ventilator. It went from 9:00 A.M. to 10:00 A.M. to 11:30 A.M. I got ten new knots in my stomach with each time change. But I still have

*the peace that passes all understanding. I don't
know what to exactly expect, but here we go…
Ashlyn was extubated today at 12:30 P.M. It
is now 8:45 P.M. She's been breathing on her
own for eight hours and fifteen minutes. She's
so sweet! She's been grinning and laughing.
She's so happy to be off of that tube. She's like
a different person.
All of the nurses are so amazed at how well
she's doing. We had the family and my pastors
here. I truly believe in divine order and God
as ordered every step today. Ash is resting
very well now and has been all evening.
Hopefully, we both can get some sleep! God
is such an AMAZING God!!! I'm really at a
loss for words. There is power in prayer that
is for sure!!!   ~KDH*

~JOURNAL ENTRY: SATURDAY, OCTOBER 9, 2010~

*Today was a good day. Ashlyn is still
hanging strong, thank God! I took pictures of
her with both of her grandmothers and they
took some with Ash and me. She even smiled
a bit for the camera.*

~JOURNAL ENTRY: WEDNESDAY, OCTOBER 13, 2010~

*It's been a tough last few days watching
Ash go through withdrawals from the all
the narcotic meds she's been on. It's really*

hard to watch. I wonder if she is having mild hallucinations and just can't verbalize it. She has not let me out of her sight. I have become her security blanket without a doubt. I've slept in the hospital bed with her for the last several nights. I can't lie and say I haven't been in a lot of pain (my back is aching like crazy), but I wouldn't trade it for the world! My baby needs me and she's gonna have me.

~JOURNAL ENTRY: FRIDAY, OCTOBER 15, 2010
"THE BIG 1:00 MEETING"~

Robert and I are meeting with Ashlyn's team of doctors to set a target date for going home...discharged from the hospital! At the end of the meeting I felt a little better about what direction we were going in and WHY the doctors felt the NEED to send her home so suddenly. Ashlyn is more at risk being in the hospital and catching more infections than being at home in a more controlled environment. Whatever the reasons, her going home was music to my ears! I keep trying to wrap my head around what is going on. God is SO AMAZING! Last week Robert and I were looking at hospice facilities and preparing to make funeral arrangements. Now, only a week after taking her off the ventilator, we are making plans to bring her home. All I say is thank you Jesus! Thank you Jesus! My prayer is that I am still open to you, Father. May

*Thy will be done and may You grant me Your
patience and peace as I walk this thing through
till the very end. In Jesus' mighty name.*

Amen.

On Wednesday, October 20, 2010, Robert and I brought
Ashlyn home from the hospital. Our girl was a born fighter
and a strong-willed warrior. I stood in amazement at all the
obstacles she successfully hurdled and the odds she defied.
She was an expert odds defying warrior. We both were.

~DETOX~

Ashlyn came home on a weaning plan after having
been on several different pain meds (heavy narcotics)
over a long period of time. The idea that a person can be
weaned off drugs with the use of other drugs (that are
just as potent) was unfathomable to me. Nevertheless,
that was the plan. We had never done it before, and was
it ever an experience.

For five days, we had to decrease her medicine in
specific dosages. Now, I'm no doctor or nurse, but common
sense serves me well. In my humble opinion, a five-day
detox from drugs that have been in the system for months
just didn't compute. I really had to watch her as we were
going through this process. Thank God I had the help of
in home nurses once again. It turned out that, on a couple
of those days, we weaned her too much and her body's
reaction (now in addiction) was in total disarray. Ashlyn
was already strong prior to the hospitalization, but the

drugs made her five times her normal strength. The look in her eyes was different. Ashlyn was not Ashlyn. She was going through narcotics withdrawals. How unfair for my innocent child to have to detox from drugs she never willingly consumed in the first place.

She physically fought me. She physically fought the nurses. Ashlyn's flailing and fighting was so bad that one nurse actually left and didn't return. One day in particular, I found myself on the floor restraining her from behind with my entire body, out of breath and rocking her from side-to-side. I had bruises all over my body. The plan was clearly not working. After calling the doctor and explaining what was going on, he agreed she needed a slower weaning method. He prescribed a fourteen-day treatment. I just wanted my daughter back to her normal state. It was an uphill battle, but we got through it.

Still uncertain of what the future would bring after this traumatic experience, it was still a wonderful feeling to have her physically home again.

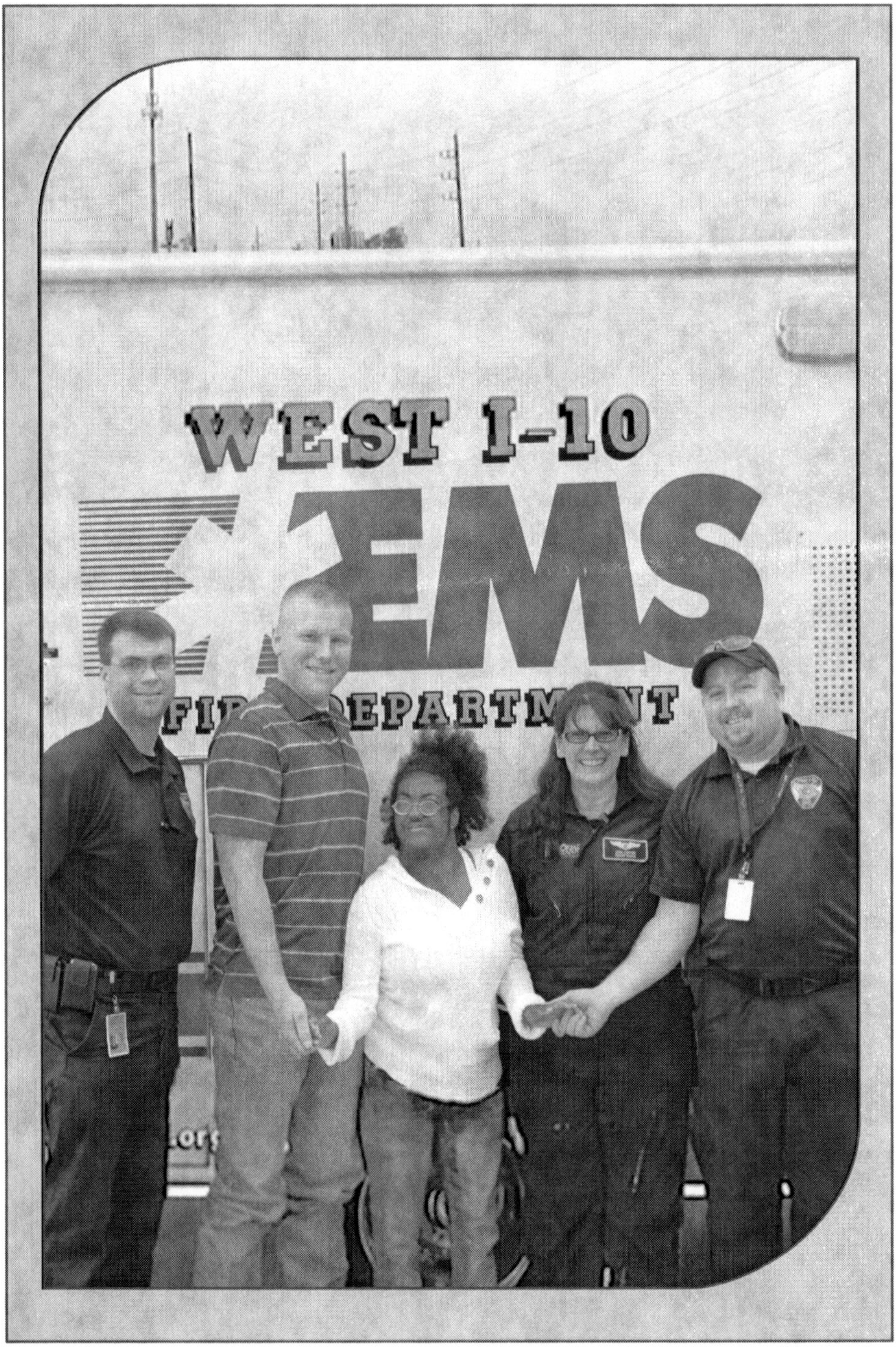
WEST I-10
EMS

CHAPTER TWELVE

THE FINAL FIGHT

*"What we once enjoyed, we can never lose. All that
we love deeply becomes part of us."*
~Hellen Keller

Fast-forward seven months. Ashlyn was making remarkable progress once all of the meds were out of her system. She immediately started back with therapy. We wasted no time where that was concerned. I remember the day I wheeled her into the building. There were gasps and tears of joy from the moms and therapists in the lobby. That smile of hers was so big. She definitely felt the love. It even put a smile on my face. I knew it would take a while to get Ashlyn back to her original baseline, and I was prepared to take the long walk with her. I just needed her to go for it. I had decided (and told Robert) that school was not even a priority on my list for Ashlyn. I withdrew her with no intention of sending her back until she was strong and healthy enough to return. That lasted three months.

In case it's not obvious, Ashlyn was a determined girl. One day, she was downstairs and crawled to the back door. She sat there looking out the window. She took her glasses off her face, threw them across the room and uttered the words "Bye-bye, M-o-m-m-a" as she continued looking out the glass door. I cried as I watched her protest and plead her case to get out of the house. I felt like I was torturing her by keeping her from what she loved most - school. Therapy and bike rides weren't enough for her. She wanted the interaction with her friends and teachers at school. It was a catch-22. Would I continue to keep her home where I could control her germ environment, or would I allow her to live her life and let her do what she loved to do? I ultimately decided to call her school and see if we could work out a plan, easing Ashlyn back into the school setting with half-days, two-to-three days a week. We had an ARD meeting because everything had to be documented. The plan was put in motion. Ashlyn began that following Monday. She was so happy!

Things, of course, were modified for her more than ever. She stayed in her handicapped stroller most of the time. She couldn't handle the long distant walks through the school anymore. I would pick her up at 11:30 A.M. on her school days, and on Tuesdays and Thursdays physical therapy was her activity. I didn't want to overexert her. We had Ashlyn on that schedule all of February, keeping a close eye on her. She seemed to be handling everything fine. Her doctor had cleared everything, and there was no respiratory distress. Ashlyn was given the green light to continue her normal school regimen prior to her hospitalization. I was happy for her.

In March, she began full, modified days at school. She did just fine. She was making progress at therapy and at school, but her physical mobility and endurance were taking awhile to come around. That concerned me.

We got through March. April 2 came, and our girl turned seventeen years old. All of Ashlyn's birthdays were a time of reflection for me. What a blessing to have conquered so many mountains, and she had been doing it with a smile on her face.

Shortly after her birthday she caught a cold. I kept her home from school. Initially, her symptoms were just a runny nose and sore throat. I took her to the doctor. The appropriate medications were prescribed. When the symptoms seemed to have cleared up I sent her back to school.

A few days had gone by and Ashlyn seemed tired in a different way than what was normal for her. I kept her home for a few days so she could regain her strength.

Robert came over to see the kids and, while lying down next to Ashlyn in her bed we both noticed a very strange breathing pattern that appeared to have come out of nowhere. Her oxygen levels were in the seventy percent range. I told Robert I was taking her to the ER. I felt on a gut level that was the thing to do. He asked, "Are you sure?" I was positive. "Yes," I said. I gathered her things. This time seemed different. There was no sense of extreme emergency. I just knew I didn't want to go to her regular pediatrician and that she needed her lungs x-rayed. Jenny, the kids' baby sitter, went with Ashlyn and me to the ER. We were assigned a room. The doctor came in immediately to assess what was going on. They realized her oxygen levels were low and put her on oxygen.

About ten minutes into having the oxygen mask on, Ashlyn went into severe respiratory distress. It came on so suddenly. Ash had an audience of ER physicians, nurses and respiratory therapists, all with surprised expressions on their faces. The dialogue shifted from, "Mom, we'll want to just keep her overnight and monitor her," to "Well, Mom we are going to intubate her and admit her to PICU immediately."

She was transported upstairs to the second floor PICU. I was told to wait in the lobby of the unit until they got Ashlyn situated in the room, and the nurse would call the lobby attendant to let me know when to come back and see her. An hour had passed and just when impatience was about to get the best of me, one of the PICU physicians came out to talk to me. I felt as though I was standing outside myself watching the scene. I was at once praying and trying to listen to the doctor. She said to me, "Mom, are you okay?" I replied, "No. What's going on? I haven't been called back yet." She told me they were having trouble getting Ashlyn stabilized. "Her (oxygen levels) began to drop drastically and she is on a higher percentage of oxygen. Are you okay?," the doctor asked. Am I okay? Was she seriously wanting an answer to that question? "No, I'm not okay. I want to go back and see my daughter." I was pretty demanding by then. Her reply was, "It shouldn't be long before they call you back." She put her hand on my back and said that if I needed anything I could let her know. I felt I was getting mixed signals from her. Or maybe there were signals I was just refusing to acknowledge.

I was finally called back to see Ashlyn. After washing my hands, I was buzzed in to go behind monitored and secured doors. While walking through the hallway, I saw bed paddles atop what I recall being a flat stainless steel rolling cart in the hallway just outside of Ashlyn's room - bed number twenty three. I asked the nurse about the paddles. I was told that while they were getting Ashlyn "situated" in her PICU room, she had indeed flat lined, but the paddles were not used. "The paddles were here in case they were needed. Medication was used to bring her back and she responded quite well," the doctor said. I felt a giant knot in my stomach. Adrenaline raced through my body. I could not believe all that was going on while I was waiting to see her. I took a few steps over to her bed and whispered in her ear, "Mommy is here, Ash. Mommy is right here. I love you." Tears began to fall as I rubbed her forehead and traced my fingers through her hair over and over. She lay there intubated (again), on oxygen (again), with an I.V. in her arm (again) and probes all over her body, which monitored her heart rate, oxygen levels, blood pressure and a host of other things (again). At a total loss for words, all I could say was, "Jesus. Jesus. Jesus."

Weeks went by. Test after test, x-ray after x-ray and med after med. I had requested several times that members of her "normal" physician team be paged. They were. I even left messages for them on their voice mails. Not a single one of them was available. Not one. That was odd to me. I later realized there was Divine order in it all. The team on board at that stage was not familiar (personally) with Ashlyn's medical history. They figured it out as they went along. One doctor even commented to me "Your daughter seems to be a very complicated little girl. She keeps us on our toes." Ashlyn was full of surprises. She would be doing well for days at a time, and then everything would take a turn for the worse. Just as suddenly, she would shift and do well again, stabilize for a week or so and then the yo-yo process would repeat itself. In the midst of the back and forth, Robert and I felt it was time to start bringing our family into town. He had been "Mr. Mom" again, taking care of Camron while I stayed at the hospital with Ashlyn. He brought me food everyday. He relieved me when I needed it. There's nothing like a hot shower when you haven't had one for days. I met the doctors every morning for their rounds so that I could ask questions and learn of any new developments.

On June 13, 2011, the doctors made their rounds as usual, but this particular morning, Ashlyn was the first patient. They congregated outside her door talking amongst themselves, and I invited myself into the meeting. What they said caught me off guard. They told me they had done all they could do for Ashlyn. "At this point, all we can do is keep her comfortable." I knew there was something different about this time.

Robert and I stayed by her side. We had been prepped by the doctors as to how things were going to happen, but nothing prepared us for what did. Her blood pressure began to drop. The nurse adjusted Ashlyn, her tubes, her I.V. and her cords so I could lie beside her in her bed. I nestled and snuggled as best I could with all the tubing. The nurse had been looking at her monitor and blurted out, "Somebody loves her Momma! Her blood pressure is going back up." Robert was rubbing her legs and covered them with blankets, hoping the warmth would be the miracle we needed to keep her with us. I whispered in her ear, "That's it Ashlyn! You fight! Mommy and Daddy are right here. We are right here."

I kept kissing and hugging her, assuring her of my love for her. Through my tears and blurred vision, I saw Robert sitting bedside rubbing her while one tear fell, then another. He told Ashlyn aloud how much daddy loved her. Of course, that made me more emotional. The two of them loved each other so much. Her father mesmerized her and I thought if she could hear him say it that may be the one thing to turn everything around.

Robert and I agreed to call the grandparents and have them come and bring Camron to the hospital. Things didn't appear to be going well. I didn't move. As far as I was concerned, they would have to bring me a bedpan or a catheter because I wasn't moving.

Ashlyn's blood pressure began to drop again. This time it dropped in bigger increments. Her heart rate did the same. I whispered in my daughter's ear for a final time, "Ash, can you do mommy one favor? Can you just tell Jesus I said 'thank you?' Thank Him for such a beautiful gift. I hope that He is pleased with the job that I did." A tear rolled from her left eye. The side closest to me. I knew beyond a shadow of a doubt that she not only heard me, but also understood me and that it wouldn't be long.

Ashlyn transitioned from her earthly life to her eternal life on June 14, 2011. It was very difficult, but beautiful to witness a life lived with such joy, purity and innocence. I learned so much in that seventeen-year journey with my daughter. I always try to live my life knowing that I have God to answer to for everything I do, but I also believe that my experience raising Ashlyn increased my standards to another level in my desire to want to be the very best person that I can be. Because of Ashlyn, I am determined that others see the Christ in me just by looking at my life...a life of service. Although my angel Ashlyn is no longer here physically, I am driven to bring awareness to the medical community and to be a resource of information to families of children with the same or similar diagnosis as Ashlyn. I am also driven to educate the world about 1p36 Deletion Syndrome through the *Ashlyn Horry Foundation*.

As that young college girl, never in a million years did I see my life as it is today. If I had been told to write the perfect love story, I couldn't have written it any better than the one that has been written for me. Ashlyn was an angel sent from heaven to give me, Robert and Camron, the rest of her family and so many others the unconditional love that can only come from a loving God. Certainly, the emotional struggles and challenges to overcome occurred almost daily, but the overall reward is the love that conquers all things, the love that endures all things, the love that believes all things.

Love never fails.

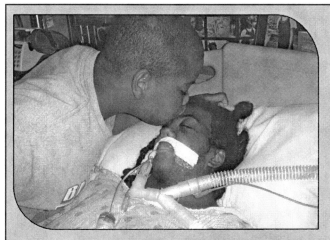

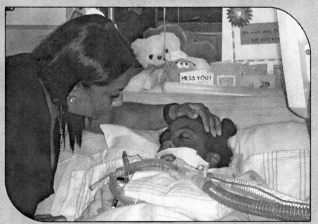

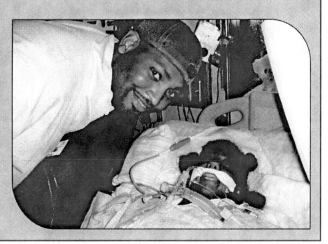

Acknowledgments

Humbled before the Almighty God, I give the utmost thanks and praise for the gift of Your son, Jesus Christ, for without Him I am nothing. Father, I am forever grateful for Your grace and mercy. But most of all, I am grateful for Your faithfulness, which has brought me to this point in my life.

Thank you Mom, for all of your love, support and prayers. You selflessly put your life aside to help me through one of the most difficult times in my life, and God knows I couldn't have gotten through without you. You gave me the ease and comfort of knowing that my children were in good hands while I focused on my healing and my writing of this book. You helped this book come to fruition. Thank you with all of my heart.

To my sister, Mikka: Thank you so much for reading my chicken scratch and helping to make this book come to life through your typing skills. They are a lot better than mine! And to my brother, Bernie: Thank you always for your unwavering love and support. You both mean the world to me and I love you dearly.

To Lelia – my "Mother-in-Law...always": I can't say thank you enough for all that you have done throughout the years. No matter what was needed, you have always made yourself available. There's a burning trail from Alabama to Texas. They should name I10 after you.

To Robert – my "Father-in-Law...always": I think my dad must have given you the nod or passed the torch to you. You have been such an amazing support to me. You've offered such strong encouragement at the times when I needed it most, and even when I didn't feel I needed it at all. You stepped right in and made such an impact in my life. And I thank you.

To my extended family - The Barr's, The Wilson's, Jenna Cooper and many others...you know who you are: Your love and support for my family and me will never go unnoticed. Thank you for always being there.

To my spiritual mentors: The late, Sue Jones, and Ladell and Gwen Graham, what would I do without you? You have kept me grounded and focused. You have been nothing less than loving, supportive and selfless. I am so thankful to have you all in my life.

To ALL the doctors, surgeons, nurses, therapists, specialists, teachers and paraprofessionals who have worked with Ashlyn or had her as a patient or student, I am forever grateful.

To my academic advisor, Ana Schuber at the University of Alabama: I appreciate everything you did to keep pushing me and believing in me when I didn't feel the prize was within reach. What started out as my Senior Project as a prerequisite for graduating, has now become a published memoir. Thank you, Ana, Cindy, Ric Dice and all of the University of Alabama EXD staff. You truly helped to make a personal goal a reality in more ways than one.

To Dee Worley, God works in mysterious ways, doesn't he? He truly uses the foolish to confound the wise. Thank you for feeling the heartbeat of this project. My hat is off to you and your professional expertise.

To Linda Roghar at White River Press, LLC: Thank you for your patience, understanding and believing in me throughout this whole project.

To the board members of *The Ashlyn Horry Foundation*: I thank you from the bottom of my heart for giving of your time and talents to serve in such a genuine and willing way. You all make a difference in the lives of others.

To the love of my life, Robert, thank you for the wonderful years and memories that we hold so dear. Most importantly, thank you for the two gifts we both treasure above all - our "rugrats."

Last but not least, to my two children, Ashlyn and Camron: I love you both more than words can express. You make Mommy's heart so full of joy. I am prayerfully grateful that you are all that God has purposed you to be.

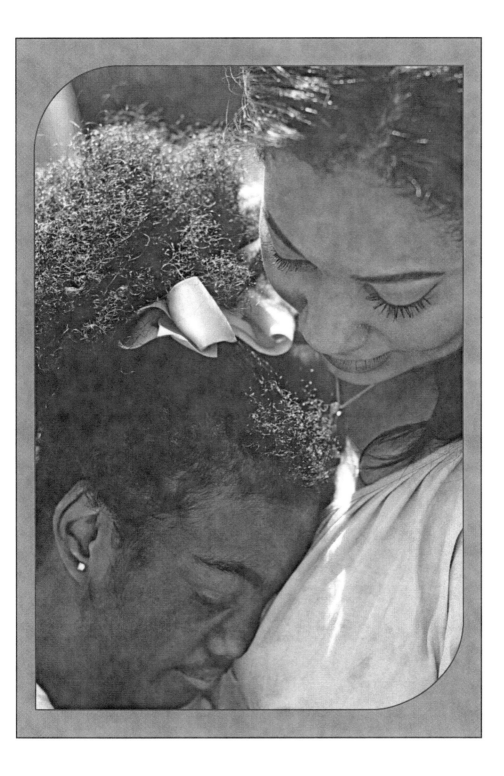

CPSIA information can be obtained at www.ICGtesting.com
Printed in the USA
LVOW040306240113

317005LV00002B/2/P